CANADIAN MODERN

"Living lightly on the earth:"
building an Ark for Prince Edward Island, 1974-76

STEVEN MANNELL

ARK DESIGNERS: **DAVID BERGMARK** AND **OLE HAMMARLUND**
OF SOLSEARCH ARCHITECTS WITH THE NEW ALCHEMY INSTITUTE

SERIES EDITOR: **MICHELANGELO SABATINO**
INTRODUCTION: **DANIEL A. BARBER**

Dalhousie Architectural Press
Faculty of Architecture and Planning
Dalhousie University
5410 Spring Garden Road, Halifax, Nova Scotia, Canada
PO Box 15000 B3H 4R2
dal.ca/archpress

Editorial Board
Essy Baniassad, Chinese University of Hong Kong / University of Botswana
Sarah Bonnemaison, Dalhousie University
Brian Carter, SUNY Buffalo
Hans Ibelings, Architecture Observer
Christine Macy, Dean and Board Chair, Dalhousie University
Frank Palermo, Dalhousie University
Michelangelo Sabatino, Illinois Institute of Technology

Series: *Canadian Modern*
ISBN: 978-0-929112-69-5
Series editor: Michelangelo Sabatino
Publications Manager: Susanne Marshall
Publications Managers (Temporary): Katie Arthur and Brad Congdon
Designer: Anthony Taaffe
Printed by Halcraft Printers.

For Laureen

© 2018 Dalhousie Architectural Press
All rights reserved. Published February 2018
Printed in Canada

Library and Archives Canada Cataloguing in Publication

Mannell, Steven, author
    "Living lightly on the earth:" building an Ark for Prince Edward Island, 1974-76 / Steven Mannell.

(Canadian modern)
Accompanies an exhibition held at the Confederation Centre of the Arts from October 15, 2016 to April 30, 2017.
Includes bibliographical references.
ISBN 978-0-929112-69-5 (paperback)

1. Sustainable buildings--Prince Edward Island--Exhibitions. 2. Sustainable architecture--Prince Edward Island--Exhibitions. 3. Prince Edward Island--Buildings, structures, etc.--Exhibitions. I. Confederation Centre of the Arts, host institution II. Title. III. Series: Canadian modern (Dalhousie Architectural Press)

TH4860.M35 2016   728'.047   C2016-906228-7

 We acknowledge the support of the Canada Council for the Arts, which last year invested $153 million to bring the arts to Canadians throughout the country.

Front cover: Nancy Willis: unknown photographer, 1977.

Conseil des arts   Canada Council
du Canada   for the Arts

CONFEDERATION
CENTRE ART GALLERY

Contents

The P.E.I. Ark

The New Alchemists

Foreword

Michelangelo Sabatino

The Ark for Prince Edward Island is one of Canada's pioneering experiments in self-sufficient "green" buildings heated by solar energy and powered by wind. Commissioned as one of Canada's contributions to the United Nations' inaugural conference on Human Settlements (Habitat '76) held in Vancouver, BC, it was heralded for its leadership role in bioshelter design. During those years, Vancouver was the epicenter of two important counterculture developments related to the environment: Greenpeace was founded in 1971 and R. Murray Schafer coined the expression "soundscape," a concept that directed new focus on the acoustic relationship of animals, humans, and the earth. On the Ark's 40th anniversary, Steven Mannell's exhibition and catalogue – *"Living lightly on the earth:" building an Ark for Prince Edward Island, 1974-76* – focuses scholarly attention by way of abundant primary sources to the ideas and know-how that underpin the Ark. Consisting of a living space, greenhouse, and laboratory on a remote natural site (Spry Point) facing the Northumberland Strait of the Gulf of St. Lawrence, the Ark flourished for a few short years before being decommissioned, partially demolished, and replaced by a neo-traditional hotel building.

Our series *Canadian Modern* focuses the attention of general and specialized audiences to significant episodes that have transformed the built and natural environments of Canada. While we acknowledge the role that nationhood can play in shaping culture, we understand architectural identity to be rather indifferent to the ideology of borders. The Ark, financed by the Canadian federal government, is especially demonstrative of the porous qualities of national identify insofar as John Todd, the Canadian biologist whose ideas frame the Ark, was trained in Canada and America; the New Alchemy Institute that guided the project was based in Cape Cod, Massachusetts; while the architect-builders – the American David Bergmark and the Dane Ole Hammarlund – were both émigrés to Canada as a direct result of the project. Thus, the Ark is a significant episode in cross-pollination of know-how and people during the 1960s and 1970s between Canada, the US, and numerous countries throughout the world. It was part of a phenomenon that witnessed an influx of new generations

0.01 "The P.E.I. Ark" poster by Solsearch Architects, ink on mylar, ca. August 1975. This poster shows the penultimate, third Ark design, which features a consolidated volume and air-based heating system. The Ark is set in a developed landscape of vegetable gardens and tree plantations, with two Hydrowind turbines and the waters of the Northumberland Strait in the distance.

of design professionals who arrived in response to the image of a multicultural can-do nation epitomized by Expo '67. Unlike today's global architects who typically visit Canada only to carry out their commissions, the influx of émigrés during the 1960s and 1970s, and those before them during the inter-war and post-war years, initiated a long-term engagement with Canadian society and its schools of architecture well beyond the initial realization. Both Bergmark and Hammarlund continue to practice in Prince Edward Island today.

In addition to addressing the implications of national identity (the adjective Canadian in our series title), our books and catalogues are also informed by research into how the ideas of modernity, modernization, and modernism informed and transformed architecture and the built environment. Through the research that we publish, we are constantly interrogating the modern(s) as it applies to the Canadian context. The Ark represents a collective response to the challenges brought by the OPEC oil crisis of 1973-78 and more generally by the excess in technological determinism and over-reliance upon finite resources used to fuel a growing addiction to the automobile and other consumer conveniences. Shortly after the publication of Rachel Carson's *Silent Spring*, Bernard Rudofsky's 1964 MoMA exhibition *Architecture without Architects* praised the "spontaneous" builders of pre-industrial vernacular traditions for their "rare good sense in the handing of practical problems." Although the principles underlying the Ark are "futuristic" insofar as they rely on forward-thinking approaches to bioshelters, its architectural language is characterized by a vernacular modern aesthetic — in this case defined by pitched roofs and a natural material palette. While contemporary architects engaged with sustainability have eschewed the low-tech aesthetics of the vernacular in favor of more high-tech expression, especially in urban settings, the aesthetic and technical legacy of the Ark continues to resonate in Canada and beyond for the courage with which it was conceived and realized.

Assessing the Ark

Daniel A. Barber

The Ark for Prince Edward Island presents a constructive and important challenge to our understanding of the history of architecture. It emerged in the mid-1970s, amid a persistent cloud of disquiet over the received imperatives of the Modern Movement in architecture. The Ark inserted itself as a thoughtful and coherent conception of architectural activity that simultaneously engaged new ideas about program, construction, and materials, and that also contributed to a re-framing of relationships between human and biotic systems.

Our historical perspective on the project is complicated by the fact that, in familiar narratives of the history of architecture, developments such as the Ark tend to be relegated to a kind of utopianism – a quest for a way of living that was simultaneously not very possible and not so desirable, often represented by various counter-cultural back-to-the-land movements that sought to isolate themselves from larger social forces in order to live differently. Recent scholarship has offered important qualifiers to this so-called "hippie modernism," both exploring its richness and suggesting, in some cases, that some of these architectural reformulations of familiar social and political structures in fact resonated widely across multiple spheres of social and cultural activity.[1]

Yet the Ark represents something else – it is not an architecture of enlightened alternatives, but an instance of designed engagement with a rich strain of governmental interest in understanding how environmental pressures can be reflected and mediated through architectural practices. As such, the Ark resonates not just through a different history of architecture, but also a different historical framework for the broad popular interest in environmentalism.

This historical revision brings us back further, to the 1940s and 1950s. The process that led to the Ark – and ultimately to the UN Conference on the Human Environment in Stockholm in 1972 – began in large part with concerns about resource scarcity immediately after World War II. Before access to the oil of the Middle East was secured, a wide range of experiments, conferences, publications, and exhibitions sparked interest in alternative means of energy production, and the shifts to lifestyle and social organization embedded within them. New ways of designing buildings, with increased attention to attenuating a structure to its environmental surround, were essential.

0.02

0.02 Looking east from the balcony in the commercial greenhouse, with Suntube fish ponds on the north, in-ground planting beds down the centre, and a raised planting bench along the south wall, Fall 1976. Grape vines climb the wooden columns.

Solar houses were built at the Massachusetts Institute of Technology and Arizona State University (then the Arizona State College), as well as in Israel, South Africa, and southern France. Experiments in climatic methods in design, inspired by architects in Brazil, West Africa, and other southern regions, began to be codified in northern laboratories and developed in strict accordance to received traditions of architectural modernism.

If architecture was the experimental medium, the effects were more wide-ranging. By the end of the 1950s, a number of non-governmental organizations emerged in order to promote the idea that different regional conditions allowed for different patterns of energy use and supply. The policy innovations – and the socio-political networks – of the global environmental movement of the 1970s were nurtured in these new technological approaches. Architecture was a central node in this distributed network focused on how to think about human participation in the global ecological system.

There were significant Canadian contributions. Maurice Strong, the Canadian energy executive who was also the secretary general of the 1972 conference in Stockholm, and then the founding director of the UN Environment Programme, represents one side of this bureaucratic contribution. The Ark, as a global project based in Canada, also reflects an environmentalism of consensus politics. Social issues were foregrounded as a networked condition of knowledge development in ways of living. The Ark was part of a wide-ranging interest in these architectural and technological strategies – less a design aesthetic, and more an experimental ethic for exploring material efficiency. The Earthships, underground houses, Appropriate Technologies, and autonomous houses that proliferated in the 1970s expand our sense of eco-aesthetics, emphasize the relational conditions of the built object, and propose a systems approach to environmental design.

Indeed, since this time, the design fields, broadly considered, have been an important site for both the *discussion* of environmental issues and the *construction* of possible pathways towards new ways of living. As the Ark demonstrates, in this discursive and conceptual impulse of cultural engagement we can see the importance of architecture to more general environmental concerns. The project reflects an orientation towards alternative forms of energy generation (solar, wind, and biomass), food production, and water recycling, finding these significant not only for their environmental and economic benefits, but also because living differently with natural systems encouraged enlightened policy-making, new forms of social organization, and advocated for local rather than the global economies.

Architectural discussions tend to use the term "environment" as part of a broader cultural imperative that frames environmentalism as a technological project to

0.03 The Ark enclosed, solar panels installed, and rough grading of the site complete, Summer 1976. The lower part of the end wall slides up the slope to open the greenhouse to the exterior.

restructure relationships between social and natural processes. However, the precise mechanisms towards social change that could be facilitated by design innovations – that could begin to move the body politic towards a different relationship with biotic systems – have often been left rather vague. This was not the case in the Ark. The social was foregrounded, and embedded in technological decisions.

In other words, in familiar frameworks of environment, the relationship between the natural and the cultural is inadequately interrogated and problematized. Architects have long had the opportunity to recognize a more complex state of affairs: that nature is "constructed" – a cultural idea that relates to the world outside but does not define it and is not adequate to it; and that culture itself is not a given, but is constantly being produced, reproduced, reimagined in the image of different futures. Insofar as we are trying to identify productive means to relate "architecture" and "environment," the relevance of the architectural discussion is in how it can serve to best articulate the specific ideas and desires embedded in a still emerging environmental culture.

The details about the Ark presented in this volume go a long way towards clarifying how these desires could have been further realized, and also suggest how they can impact design practice today. The Ark came at a crucial time. It was a robust example of an architectural project that clarified new policy priorities at a moment when governmental environmental policies were shifting towards an anti-regulation, privatization-focused neoliberal approach. The Ark demonstrated that cultural desires could, through architecture, be brought into public view in dramatic and substantive ways. Indeed, this implicit reformulation of *the public*, as distinct from governance, as the site for technological innovation and social progress, is perhaps the strongest legacy of this compelling architectural event.

0.04

0.04 Looking towards the Ark from the northwest, across a field of buckwheat, 1977. The Hydrowind turbine is at the left.

The Ark Moment:
Celebrating an Ecological Dreamscape

At midday on September 20, 1976, two helicopters descended on Spry Point, Prince Edward Island, landing amidst a crowd of several hundred rural Islanders, counterculture youth, alternative technology proponents, and assorted curiosity seekers. Canadian Prime Minister Pierre Trudeau and Island Premier Alex Campbell had arrived to open the Ark for Prince Edward Island. Trudeau and Campbell were greeted by two young girls bearing bouquets of wildflowers, and led through a throng of children and reporters along a path through the grass to the porch at the western end of the Ark building for the official ceremony.

This "Ark" that the politicians had come to welcome to the Island's shore was not a boat but a building: a modest-sized building at that, not much larger than a house. It might have seemed a humble structure to attract the official helicopters of the Prime Minister, and indeed it was more than just a building. Like the biblical Noah's Ark, it hosted a menagerie of life forms intended to populate a world in recovery from catastrophe, and it embodied a new covenant for an ethical approach to living. Its architecture of glass volumes and clapboard sheds evoked associations with everything from old barns to space stations, aptly expressing the mix of advanced research and traditional common-sense that informed its principles.[1] According to its designers,

> The Ark is an ecologically designed bioshelter powered and heated by the wind and sun. It houses a research laboratory, living unit, family garden and a small commercial greenhouse and fish farm. The structure is experimental, exploring new ideas in self-sufficiency, in biological systems, and in intensive food production. The ultimate goal is to create shelters that sustain and support their inhabitants.[2]

The Ark was part of a flowering of ecological design projects in the 1970s, nurtured by the counterculture youth movements of the 1960s, the international activism leading

1.01 The Ark for Prince Edward Island, Spry Point, Little Pond, near Souris, PE, designed by Solsearch Architects and the New Alchemy Institute, 1974-76. Architects David Bergmark and Ole Hammarlund, principals of Solsearch Architects, at the southeast corner of the Ark for Prince Edward Island, Fall 1976.

1.02 High technology brings political leaders to celebrate Appropriate Technology, as Prime Minister Pierre Trudeau's helicopter descends on the Ark for the official opening ceremony, September 1976.
1.03 John Todd and Island Premier Alex Campbell flank Prime Minister Trudeau, with Nancy Jack Todd, Nooni Hammarlund (in braids), and Chris Willis (blue jacket) just in front.

to the first Earth Day in 1970, and anti-war and anti-nuclear resistance triggered by the Cold War, Vietnam, and the advent of commercial nuclear power. Initially ignored by governments and professionals, this new "ecological architecture" received a rush of official attention, funding, and opportunities during the OPEC oil crisis of 1973–80. The Ark can be understood as an early essay in ecological architecture. While conventional buildings sought to shelter their inhabitants from the surroundings, providing an artificially maintained "inside" set apart from the "outside," the Ark embraced the natural processes of its setting, using sun, wind, and biology to create an integrated interior and exterior ecosystem. Natural processes using renewable sources took the place of burning fossil fuels, and cultivation supplanted consumption in providing for the inhabitants' needs.[3]

Less than two years before the opening day, the Canadian and Island governments had invited the New Alchemy Institute, a collective of scientists and humanists committed "to restore the lands, protect the seas, and inform the earth's stewards," to construct the Ark as a demonstration of an alternative path for energy and development.[4] Since 1967, Premier Campbell's provincial government had embraced E.F. Schumacher's "Small is Beautiful" approach to technology and economic development as a guide to a sustainable future for the Island; in the early 1970s Campbell was able to draw the interest of Pierre Trudeau's national government, along with substantial financial and scientific support.[5] In turn, Trudeau planned to showcase the Ark to the world at the United Nations Habitat '76 conference in Vancouver.[6] The New Alchemists, led by biologist John Todd, drew upon years of living experiments carried out at their farmstead on Cape Cod, Massachusetts, part of a worldwide exploration of Appropriate Technology and alternative lifestyles. Solsearch Architects of Cambridge, MA, a partnership of recent graduates David Bergmark and Ole Hammarlund, brought a synthesizing spatial vision to the assembly of techniques and ecosystems. The resulting design, construction, and operation of the Ark for Prince Edward Island was a creative collaboration of official culture with the counterculture, offering a vision of a life in collaboration with nature, free from the uncertainties of imported oil and the menace of nuclear energy.

The New Alchemists referred to the Ark as a "bioshelter," a fully self-sufficient living unit for a family of four that would provide all food and manage all wastes, using the sun and wind as energy sources. The Ark stretched east-west across its site in the form of a long, narrow prism of wood and glass. Its south face was devoted to a full-length greenhouse; on its north face, three connected sheds clad in wood siding and metal roofing stepped up in height from east to west. The tallest volume projected slightly past the west end of the greenhouse, its southwest corner hollowed out to shelter the entry beneath an upper-level balcony. The entry deck extended beyond the shelter to form a wooden bridge that floated across to meet the ground, like a gangplank.

It was on this porch that Trudeau, Campbell, and their entourage ended their trek from the helicopters. A crowd filled the balcony above and hundreds more gathered on the slope. Premier Campbell outlined the Island's hopes. John Todd described the New Alchemists' vision of the Ark and its suitability to the place:

> Here where the sea and the land and the wind and the sky come together there is a sense of place and there is a sense of the past. There is a sense of what we have and our own limits. Perhaps it's through the sense of place and past that we can begin to design and create for the 21st century.[7]

1.04

But it was Trudeau's speech that would prove most resonant with the people on site and with those who read about it in newspapers, heard it on the radio, and viewed it on television. He began with a rhetorical question:

> Distinguished guests, ladies and gentlemen. Those who are concerned about the future of mankind are haunted by three questions: will there be enough food, will we have enough energy, and can we produce both without making the earth a place which is not good to live upon? … The Ark is answering 'Yes!' to those three questions. And that is why I consider it a very exciting moment [for Prince Edward Island] where agriculture, where fisheries are so important to the livelihood of the people; where a sense of community prevails; and particularly, an island which has proven receptive to new ideas.
>
> More than one hundred years ago, the idea of confederation was developed here, and now I like to think that this Island, which has shown hospitality to this political idea which created Canada, is now providing hospitality to a new commitment: a commitment that environmentalists refer to – and I think it's a beautiful phrase – as "living lightly on the earth." I like to think that Prince Edward Island, the experience of the Ark, and all those connected with it, will be at the birth of this new commitment, of the new philosophy which we will be able then to call a technology.[8]

1.05

For Trudeau, the appropriateness of the Ark extended beyond Canada's smallest province, and he used the resonance of national history to insist on the meaning of the Ark to all humanity. J. Baldwin, a leading figure in the Appropriate Technology world, was in the crowd. He was struck by the hope that filled the gathering, the cohesion the project had brought to so many diverse people, and the way forward suggested by the success of the day. He was amazed that the Prime Minister and Premier were there with no secret service or police anywhere; and even more amazed that "the speeches

1.04 John Todd addresses the crowd from the deck at the southwest corner of the Ark dwelling unit.
1.05 Members of the Spry Point community listen to Prime Minister Trudeau's speech celebrating the Ark's commitment to "living lightly on the earth."

actually have content! People nod. There's hope in all this crazy stuff. If it works, it'll be good for PEI, and that's not all of it either.... "[9]

The Ark Community Celebrates

A lengthy and detailed official tour followed the speeches. Each part of the Ark had a team of New Alchemists standing by, who responded to insightful and appreciative questions from the dignitaries regarding the systems, the challenges, and the potentials. At the end of the tour, Trudeau offered a deeply personal response: "This is how Margaret and I would hope to live."[10] While the New Alchemists toured the official party, their Spry Point neighbours kept the crowd entertained and fed. "Our neighbours Tommy Banks and Ethel Blackett sang and played for everyone. Others of our neighbours had prepared refreshments."[11] Blackett sang with her hair in curlers, covered by a plastic kerchief, claiming she was saving her hairdo for the evening party.[12] Trudeau mingled with the crowd but left in his helicopter for another event, before the wild rumpus began. The New Alchemists welcomed the gift of celebration they received from the Spry Point gathering. "Our neighbours provided the music and everyone danced with everyone – kids and government officials, hippies and farmers and professors – all jounced about the packed living room until after midnight."[13] Baldwin reported that "the local people stay into the wee hours of the morning, drinking and making music. The premier returns, and whoops it up too. Everyone is exhausted, proud and happy and there is a very good feeling in the air. The local people refer to the project as 'our Ark.'"[14]

New Alchemist Nancy Jack Todd reflected,

> It was clear that Mr Trudeau understood the implications of what we were trying to do. He read aloud the words on the plaque that dedicates the Ark and in doing so placed it into time. The bioshelter became a reality. … It is impossible for any of us to be objective, but to have been there and noted Mr Trudeau's flexibility and his grasp of the ideas embodied in the Ark was heartening.[15]

Stewart Brand, compiler of the *Whole Earth Catalog*, added, "I'm not sure it needs to be said, but the opening of the Ark was in fact a moving – even triumphant – occasion. Such events usually aren't. This was. Like fiddle music for dancing."[16] Arthur Cordell of the Science Council of Canada saw the Ark as a beacon of possibility: "As the Ark is to PEI, so PEI can be to Canada, so Canada can be to the rest of the world."[17] Mainstream culture also took note, with extensive coverage of the Ark's opening in mass media. Under the headline "Urgent Preparations for the Future," the *Globe and Mail* expanded on Trudeau's remark that the Ark's opening was "a very important moment in the history of our country," declaring in its editorial that "without risk of hyperbole, Mr Trudeau

1.06 Prime Minister Trudeau, John Todd, and reporters in the commercial greenhouse during the tour of the Ark.
1.07 A proper Island celebration of the Ark, as Spry Point neighbour Tommy Banks plays fiddle for the crowd while the official party tours the Ark.

could have called it a very important moment in the history of our planet.... The Ark, and other experiments like it, are our first gestures of affirmation."[18]

The significance of the Ark's opening day – a national leader embracing their ideas, and supporting their realization – was a powerful affirmation for those devoted to the challenge of "living lightly on the earth," and who dared to believe that these efforts might inspire real change in North America's dominant consumer culture. Social philosopher William Irwin Thompson, founder of the Lindisfarne Association, claimed that Trudeau had performed the most significant act by a major political figure in the 1970s.[19] At Spry Point, counterculture came together with official and local cultures to imagine and build the Ark, and to celebrate the tangible vision of a better future it foretold.

1.08

1.09

1.10

1.08 Ethel Blackett sings for the crowd during the official tour. Blackett would later work as the Ark's cleaner and maintenance person.
1.09 Prime Minister Trudeau speaks with young Spry Point neighbor Andrew MacDonald.
1.10 Aerial view of the final Ark design, drawing by Ole Hammarlund, Solsearch Architects, ink on mylar, Fall 1976. The drawing exaggerates the transparency of the acrylic greenhouse roof to show the intimacy of the dwelling, dining, and kitchen areas with the adjacent kitchen greenhouse.

Form, Space, and Systems of the Ark

> THE ARK: An early exploration in weaving together the sun, wind, biology and
> architecture for the benefit of humanity. [20]

So reads the dedication signed by Prime Minister Pierre Trudeau at the Ark's opening
ceremony. This "weaving together" was accomplished in a futuristic work of ecological
architecture, with the building serving as the primary energy collector to support the
biological ecosystem contained within. The stark contrast of the two sides of the building
– glass to the south, wood to the north – demonstrated the primary objectives of the
Ark: maximum exposure to the sun and maximum protection from the wind. The solar
strategy of minimizing energy needs and maximizing energy harvest informed every
design decision, from site strategy to building detail. The Ark nestled into the slope of the
site to reduce exposed surface area, its highly insulated walls and roof minimized heat
losses, and its earth berm and tree plantings provided shelter from the cold north winds.

Architectural form was intertwined with systems both physical (solar and wind
energy) and biological (food production and waste management). In the Ark, there was
no simple distinction between the architectural envelope and the activities it enclosed:

solar energy was used simultaneously for photosynthesis and for heat and ventilation, the food-growing media of water and soil also stored and exchanged heat with the space around them, and wastes from one system (heat and biological) were used as feedstock for another (energy and nutrients). The human inhabitants of the Ark managed the interplay of systems, enjoying the harvest of food systems while contributing their own wastes as compost. Only grey water from the sinks and laundry escaped the Ark's nutrient cycle, being directed to a dry well on site.

Building Form and Composition

The usual approach to the Ark (for those not arriving by helicopter), was from the north, along a gravel road that offered a view of the low huddle of sheds hunkered into the ground, partly screened by trees, with the sea visible in the distance. The sheds extended from east to west like nested segments of a telescope: first, a sloped surface of metal roofing buttressed the greenhouse at the east end; then a low wood-clad wall and metal roof housed the barn; next a recessed porch sheltered the public entrance; and finally a tall wood wall topped by a sloped metal roof enclosed the firewood storage, with the dwelling unit behind. At the west end, the land sloped down to the south, lending additional prominence to the taller dwelling wing of the Ark.

Along the south side, a vast faceted glass surface opened up to the sun. Its mixture of light and dark, transparency and reflection, resulted from the various roles of glazing in the energy system. The lower portion was a transparent wedge of greenhouse that ran the full length of the Ark; above this was a vertical "billboard" of 36 dark glass-clad solar panels.[21] Near the west end, these solar panels stepped up slightly to make room for another series of sloped solar panels above the family garden greenhouse. This higher bank of panels denoted the extent of the living unit, which was also marked by a recessed doorway in the south greenhouse wall. To the east of this doorway was a commercial greenhouse and fish farm, while to the west, a small family garden greenhouse connected to the kitchen, serving the day-to-day needs of the resident family of four.

A 1976 design drawing shows an aerial view of the compound from the southwest, with the Ark's porch and dwelling unit in the foreground and the long face of the greenhouse stretching away to the east. This sketch portrays the active life of the building, with vent windows open and glimpses through the transparent roof to the planting beds and fish tanks within; gardens and landscape elements animate the ground around the building. Emphasis is placed on the solar panels and greenhouse. Only the end wall displays the conventions of domestic architecture, with its diagonal board siding, flat board trim edges and window surrounds, wood decks, and balcony railings

1.11 Aerial photograph of the Ark for PEI from the south, 1976. Every part of the south face of the Ark is active in energy harvest.

The P.E.I. Ark

LOCATION:
NEW ALCHEMY INSTITUTE CENTER,
LITTLE POND,
PRINCE EDWARD ISLAND,
CANADA

WINDMILL
POWER PLANT.
THE HYDROWIND GENERATING
PLANT PRODUCES 7 KW OF POWER IN
25 MPH WIND. IT USES HYDRAULICS FOR
ENERGY TRANSFER AND BLADE POSITIONING
PROVIDING ELECTRICITY TO THE ARK.
EXCESS POWER WILL BE CONTRIBUTED TO
THE PROVINCIAL POWER NETWORK.
DEVELOPMENT AND CONTINUING
RESEARCH BY NEW ALCHEMY
INSTITUTE.

GREENHOUSE HEATING AND STORAGE:
SOLAR COLLECTION: 2000 # OF GREENHOUSE
GLAZING ANGLED TO SOUTHERN SKY.
STORAGE: 118 YARD ROCKSTORAGE BEHIND GREENHOUSE
AND 15000 GALLON LIGHT TRANSPARENT WARM WATER
FISH CULTURE FACILITY. EMERGENCY HEAT:
RESISTANCE COILS IN AIR DUCTS.

RESIDENTIAL HEATING AND STORAGE:
SOLAR COLLECTION: 980 # FLAT PLATE WATER
SELECTIVE BLACK. STORAGE: 16000 GALLON
TANKS UNDER LIVING ROOM.
DISTRIBUTION: FANCOILS
SUPPLEMENTAL: WOODSTOVE
AND HYDROWIND
POWER PLANT.

THE ARK
IS AN
ECOLOGICALLY
DESIGNED BIOSHELTER
POWERED AND HEATED BY
THE WIND AND SUN. IT HOUSES
A RESEARCH LABORATORY, LIVING
UNIT, FAMILY GARDEN AND A SMALL
COMMERCIAL GREENHOUSE AND
FISH FARM. THE STRUCTURE IS
EXPERIMENTAL, EXPLORING NEW IDEAS
IN SELF SUFFICIENCY, IN
BIOLOGICAL SYSTEMS, AND IN
INTENSIVE FOOD PRODUCTION.
THE ULTIMATE GOAL IS TO
CREATE SHELTERS THAT
SUSTAIN AND
SUPPORT THEIR
INHABITANTS.

CONCEPTS

NEW ALCHEMY INSTITUTE
SPRY POINT, LITTLE POND
SOURIS R. R. 4
P.E.I. CANADA COA 2B0

NEW ALCHEMY INSTITUTE
BOX 432, WOODS HOLE
MA 02543, U.S.A.

DESIGN

SOLSEARCH ARCHITECTS
126 RICHMOND ST.
CHARLOTTETOWN
P.E.I. CANADA

SOLSEARCH ARCHITECTS
M50 MASS. AVENUE
CAMBRIDGE
MASS. 02138 U.S.A.

SUPPORT:
MINISTRY OF STATE FOR URBAN AFFAIRS
OTTAWA, CANADA
AND
THE PROVINCE OF PRINCE EDWARD ISLAND
AND
THE NEW ALCHEMY INSTITUTE

SCIENCE & AUTHORITY
ADVANCED CONCEPTS
ENVIRONMENT CANADA

The New Alchemists

— what architect Ole Hammarlund calls a "modern carpenter gothic" typical of 1970s residential architecture. In the distance, to the northeast, are two whirling "Hydrowind" windmill generators, and beyond them the sea, with people on the beach. Solsearch Architects later incorporated this sketch in an evocative two-colour poster of the PEI Ark, available by mail order for $1.50. Although it was not published until well after the opening day, the poster would have been a perfect souvenir, with its mix of technical description, architectural visualization, and biomorphic-psychedelic fonts and borders. It was widely distributed and became an iconic representation of the project.

Not obvious from photographs but hinted at in the cutaway drawings also featured on the poster, was an advanced building envelope designed to minimize winter heat loss. The Ark's metal-clad roof structure held 24 inches of fibreglass insulation. Its unusually deep 2x6 stud walls were filled with fibreglass, behind the cedar siding were layers of one-inch polystyrene foam insulation over fibreboard to reduce thermal bridging, and its exposed foundation walls were protected by two inches of foam.[22] Six-mil polyethylene with lapped and caulked joints ensured airtightness. The insulation and airtightness values far exceeded the norms of the 1970s, and anticipated the requirements of the National Energy Code of Canada for Buildings 2015.[23]

Greenhouse Systems

The Ark's greenhouse housed an ecosystem of plant and fish cultivation, which also served as a solar heating system. A sloped roof of insulating acrylic panels transmitted solar energy for both photosynthesis and passive heat gain. In heating seasons, a duct and fan drew air continuously from the peak of the greenhouse down through a rock vault under the barn, then back to a distribution duct under the planting bench at the south wall, creating a "thermal flywheel" that heated the rock and cooled the greenhouse by day, then reversed the heat flow (but not the airflow) at night.[24] Solar heat was passively absorbed by water and algae in the aquaculture tanks and by the deep soil planting beds, which returned heat to the air when the ambient air temperature was low. John Todd described these tanks as "low temperature solar furnaces."[25] The rock vault, soil planting beds, and aquaculture tanks of the greenhouse provided sufficient thermal mass to maintain productive temperatures during cold, overcast winter weather. The wood-burning backup boiler was never used.

New Alchemy's agri/aquaculture approach sought to maximize the food energy produced using solar and biological energy, while minimizing other external energy inputs. In their words, "cultural practices will thus be as close as possible to those of Mother Nature in an environment controlled by man's design and technology."[26] Deep

1.12 "The P.E.I. Ark" poster designed by Solsearch Architects, two-colour offset print, Fall 1976.
The poster gives an overview of the Ark concept, form, and systems. It was an insert in the *Journal of the New Alchemists* 4, 1977, and available by mail order.

Ark for PEI construction drawings, Solsearch Architects, pencil on mylar, dated October 1975 (actual date Fall 1976). These drawings document the construction and details as built. Though dated October 1975, just before the start of work on site, the drawings were actually made in the Fall of 1976 after the Ark was complete, and included in the Final Report to the federal government submitted in December.

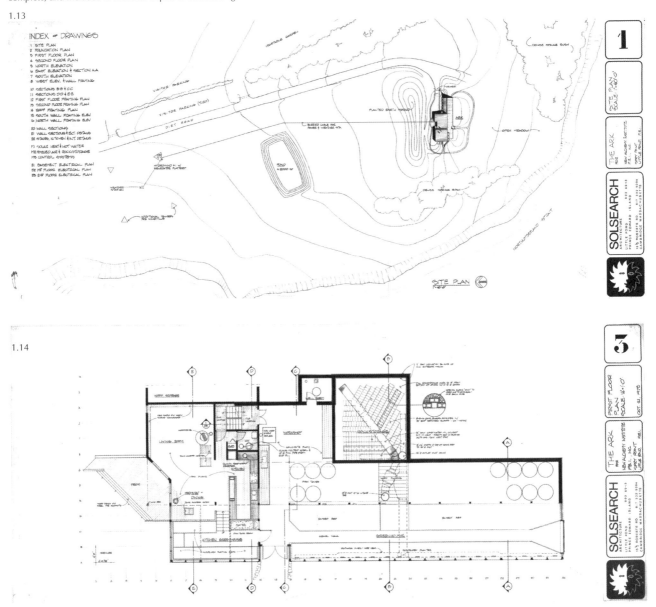

1.13 "Site Plan," scale 1 inch = 40 feet, showing the east-west orientation of the Ark. Two areas of "dense spruce bush" shelter the building from cold onshore winds, and the "planted earth mound" provides shelter from north winter winds. Earth for the mound was taken from the pond that sits midway between the Ark and the Hydrowind turbine.

1.14 "First Floor Plan," scale 1 inch = 4 feet. The kitchen greenhouse at left is open to the dining and kitchen areas, with an herb planter set into the kitchen counter at the south increasing the sense of intimacy between food production, preparation, and consumption. The commercial greenhouse on the right has a raised planting bench at the south wall, deep-soil planting beds down the centre, and two rows of "Suntube" solar fish ponds under the slope of the north roof.

1.15

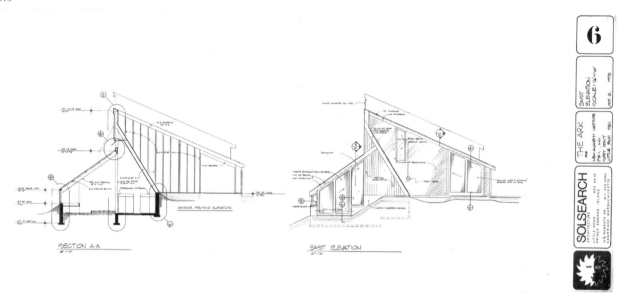

1.16

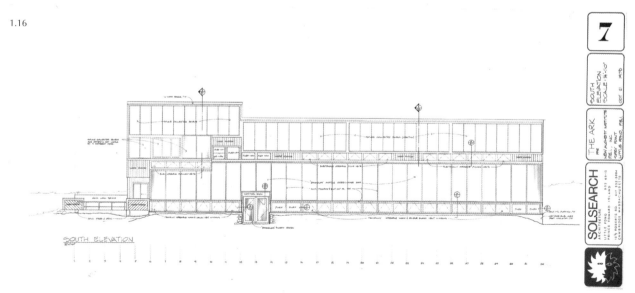

1.15 "East Elevation," scale 1 inch = 4 feet. Section A-A shows the idealized greenhouse configuration, with a sloped acrylic greenhouse roof on the south and a steeply-sloped insulated roof on the north. The interior surface of the north roof is angled and painted white to reflect low winter sun onto the fish ponds and planting beds.

1.16 "South Elevation," scale 1 inch = 4 feet. The south face of the Ark is covered in a diverse set of glazed surfaces to maximize the harvest of solar energy, used for both building energy needs and for the agri-aquaculture systems of the greenhouse.

SECTION @ BARN, ROCKSTORAGE & GREENHOUSE

1.17 "Section @ Barn, Rockstorage & Greenhouse," Ark for PEI presentation drawing, scale 1 inch = 4 feet. Solsearch Architects, ink on mylar, dated October 1975 (actual date Fall 1976). The barn and loft are on the left, above the rock vault; the commercial greenhouse is on the right. In the centre, the fan below the floor draws solar-heated air from the high point of the greenhouse into the round metal duct, then down and into the rock vault where the heat is stored. "Suntube" solar fish ponds are to the north, with deep soil planting beds and the planting bench along the south wall.

1.18 Model and diagrams of the Ark for PEI by Patrick Lefebvre, 2016-17. Cutaway plan view of the main level of the Ark, indicating the major elements.

1.19 Cutaway section view of the Ark dwelling unit and kitchen greenhouse, showing the components of the energy system.

1.20 Cutaway section view of the Ark barn, rock vault and commercial greenhouse, showing the components of the energy system.

1.18

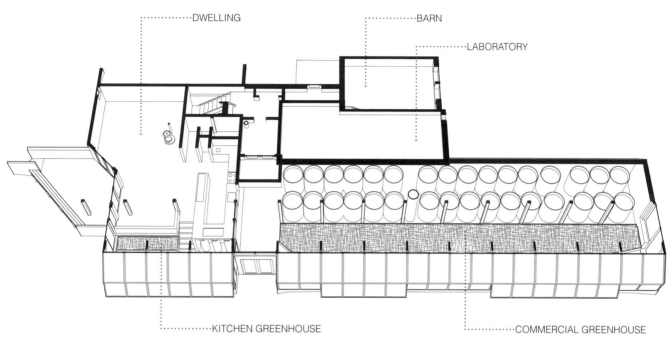

DWELLING

BARN

LABORATORY

KITCHEN GREENHOUSE

COMMERCIAL GREENHOUSE

1.19

WOOD STOVE

SOLAR PANELS FOR HEATING

SOLAR PANELS FOR HOT WATER

SOLAR COLLECTOR
WATER STORAGE TANK

VENTS

1.20

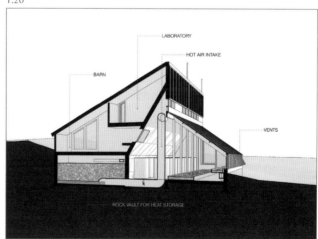

LABORATORY

HOT AIR INTAKE

BARN

VENTS

ROCK VAULT FOR HEAT STORAGE

1.21

1.22

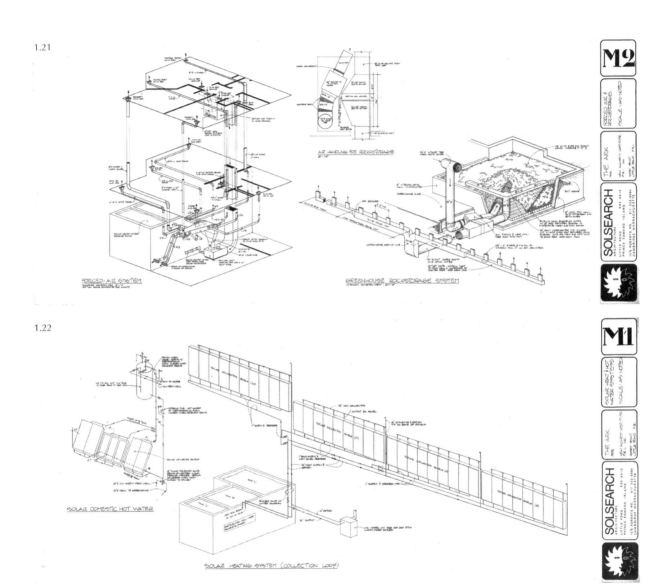

1.21 "Forced Air & Rockstorage." Left, the water storage tanks under the dwelling and the heat exchanger and air distribution system. Right, the metal duct and fan harvest solar-heated air from the greenhouse peak, the rock heat storage vault, and the distribution ducts back to the greenhouse.

1.22 "Solar Heat & Hot Water Systems." Left, the domestic water system with sloped solar collector panels. Right, the four-part "billboard" of solar collector panels serves the three-chamber water heat storage tank in the basement. Each chamber provides a different time cycle of heat storage and discharge.

soil planting beds hosted a biodiverse soil system containing nematodes, insects, and bacteria. Weeds and plant thinnings were fed to the fish or composted. No chemical fertilizers or pesticides were used, in part due to the potential effects on fish, leading to the use of disease-resistant plants and natural pest predators: lizards, spiders, ladybugs, and wasps. Instead, composted kitchen and toilet wastes and nitrogen-rich water from the fish tanks enhanced the soil fertility, augmented by seaweed harvested from the shore.

The aquaculture system used 30 cylindrical "Suntube" solar pond fish tanks, each holding 500 to 700 gallons, providing high-quality animal protein at a much lower energy cost than farm animals. Tilapia, a low-maintenance South American fish known for its rapid reproductive cycle, also had the advantage of being a non-invasive species; any escaped fish would not survive in the cool local waters. The tilapia grew rapidly amid dense, nearly black blooms of algae which, along with bacteria and plants, metabolized much of the fish waste. Only a minimal amount of fresh water entered the system, which retained heat within the tanks. The algae growth fed the fish population, and at the same time greatly enhanced the ponds' capacity to absorb and re-radiate solar energy, allowing them to serve as solar furnaces. Tanks were sheltered from overhead summer sun beneath a sloping north wall, which also reflected the low winter sun. Different tanks performed particular functions in the constructed ecosystem: some for fish, some for zooplankton production, others to cleanse the water.[27] Once established, the system was largely self-tending, beyond feeding and harvesting the fish. The New Alchemists later noted, "visitors … are often disappointed that there is nothing they can 'do' for the fish."[28]

The Living Unit Systems

A "billboard" of active solar collectors crowned the full width of the Ark, arranged vertically to maximize solar gain in December and early January when the energy need was most acute. The low sun angle, the imperative to avoid any snow accumulation, and the potential gains from sunlight reflected upwards off the surfaces of snow-covered ground and the sea beyond, made the vertical orientation optimal. Each panel was a single pane of clear optical glass over low emissivity black copper plates and water pipes which harvested solar energy. Heated water was stored in three linked insulated tanks below the living unit. A small tank served day-to-day heating demands, while two larger tanks provided seasonal storage for the winter months. A water-to-air heat exchanger and fan provided hot air to the living unit. A small woodstove served as emergency backup and, more importantly, offered local, responsive supplemental heat to the living unit. A small bank of solar panels, sloped for year-round heat collection, provided domestic hot water.

1.23

1.24

1.23 Work desk and monitoring equipment in the laboratory, with an interior window overlooking the commercial greenhouse.
1.24 Ark children in the living room, 1977. From left: Marc Hammarlund, Shira Hammarlund, Meredith Willis, Nooni Hammarlund, and Erik Hammarlund (standing). The high-efficiency Jøtul stove provided comforting direct radiant heat on-demand to supplement the passive solar system.

1.25

1.26

1.27

1.25 The commercial greenhouse looking eastwards from just inside the door from the kitchen greenhouse.
1.26 Looking from the Laboratory balcony to the commercial greenhouse, showing the white reflective surface of the north roof, along with the heat harvest duct and the ranks of solar fish ponds.
1.27 The Hydrowind turbine, Fall 1976. The tower-mounted turbine drove a hydraulic pump, which powered a generator on the ground. Excess electricity was fed into the Island grid; the grid made up power shortfalls in times of low wind.

Overall, the Ark's integrated heating and climate systems were articulated as four sub-systems, each with a specific heat management time scale:

- Hot water flat plate solar collector "billboard" and water storage tanks – long-term (multi-seasonal) storage;
- "Suntube" solar ponds – medium-term (multi-day) storage;
- Greenhouse rock storage "heat flywheel" – short-term (day to night) storage;
- Wood stove – immediate heat supply.[29]

Hydrowind Wind Energy

The Ark poster shows windmills sketched in the distance, suggesting their independence from the integrated systems of the Ark, although wind-powered electricity was crucial to the overall goal of energy self-sufficiency. The variable-pitch blades of the Ark's "Hydrowind" windmill drove a hydraulic pump. Heavy generating equipment was thus kept on the ground, and several Hydrowind mills could drive a single generator.[30] DC power from the generator was fed to an AC inverter in the Ark, providing power to run "normal household appliances" and pumps. Because the Ark was connected to the Island's electrical grid, the Hydrowind was able to feed surplus power back into the grid, rather than requiring on-site storage in batteries. The single 7.5 kW Hydrowind installed at the time of the opening met only part of the Ark's peak demand, the rest coming from the grid. New Alchemy's ambitions for Hydrowind extended well beyond the Ark; they envisioned their wind power as a nuclear- and fossil fuel-free solution to the electricity needs of the entire Island.

Living in the Ark: Human Inhabitants as Part of the Ecosystem

The Ark's weave of systems included people, with a family living on site and commuting scientists forming "an integral part of the total physical and biological system."[31] In the simplest biological terms, this meant that human wastes from kitchen and toilet, along with other organic wastes, dropped through vertical chutes into a fibreglass *Clivus Multrum* composting chamber in the basement, where slow aerobic decomposition yielded several hundred pounds of rich fertilizer each year for greenhouse plants. Composting avoided contamination of groundwater by human waste, and retained energy and nutrients within the overall Ark ecosystem.

The Ark's inhabitants were essential to the building's operation. In return, the Ark offered more than just food and warmth; the New Alchemists believed that the Ark's inhabitants would gain enlightenment and meaning through learning to build a symbiotic relationship with nature. David Bergmark of Solsearch Architects, New Alchemist Nancy Willis, and Nancy's children Chris and Meredith were the Ark's integrated "family of four," an apt symbol of the intimacy of collaborations that brought the Ark into being.[32] Over the next 18 months of the "living experiment," the family tended to the Ark's energy, food, and waste systems. Willis was the Ark's Manager, overseeing the operation of the building and tending its food systems. Contemporary film footage shows her cultivating seedlings in the planting bench, weeding leafy greens in the deep soil beds, and dropping the weeds and cuttings in the solar fish ponds. A watering can dipped into a pond provided nutrient-rich water to the plants. Children took part in all aspects of running the food systems, and family life – chores and lessons and playtime – took place surrounded by sunlight, plants, and fish. A favourite reading spot was the wood platform beside the warm air duct delivering heat from the greenhouse ridge. Bergmark worked from a drafting board set in the loft overlooking the commercial greenhouse, or in the upper-level office monitoring and logging the data from the various system sensors. The commercial greenhouse was the centre of the working life of the Ark. By opening the sliding east wall and the vent windows at top and bottom of the sloped roof, the space became part of the outside world, connecting the family to their surroundings. By spring of 1977, they completed an extension of the vegetable beds to the south-facing slope outside the greenhouse.[33]

1.28 "Space-Age Ark – Brave New Home,"
Chatelaine magazine, November 1977, 52-53.
Constance Mungall's story of spending a
February week in the Ark inspired Canadian
women to imagine the potentially liberating
joys of bioshelter life.
1.29 Looking from the kitchen and dining room to
the kitchen greenhouse, 1977. The planting bed
set into the kitchen counter enhances the sensory
intimacy between these spaces.

The heart of the Ark's family life was a big farmhouse table in the kitchen-dining area. This was adjacent to the kitchen greenhouse with its seasonal vegetables, hanging gardens, and fish tanks. A planter of herbs set into the kitchen counter shows an easy intimacy between food production and consumption. According to the New Alchemists, "the increased interior light, which in fall and early winter permeates the rooms to create a feeling of warmth, is a genuine bonus resulting from integrating living with growing areas in the Ark."[34] Everyday life was lived in a multi-sensory connection to food production, with views of greenery and fish enhanced by warmth, humidity, and aromas from activities such as cutting herbs and picking tomatoes. This connection of kitchen and table to food production remains the most compelling poetic vision of the Ark. As Constance Mungall wrote in *Chatelaine* magazine,

> At the Ark, we couldn't escape the knowledge that we depended on nature for our comfort – for the warmth of our bedrooms at night and for our work during the day, for the lettuce we picked for lunch and the broccoli for dinner. We got high on the thought that we were working with the wind and weather to form our own mini-environment, instead of depending on anonymous utilities to do that for us. And we felt good about our fellows who were working with us.[35]

Mungall and her son Alex spent a stormy week in the Ark in February 1977, among the flood of journalists and the curious who journeyed to Spry Point.

Hospitality became a major function of the Ark family. Bergmark said at the time that one of the best things about living in the Ark was the chance to talk to so many people who were interested in some aspect of it.[36] Spry Point neighbours continued to drop in. Some food systems researchers who regularly worked in the Ark lived off site; other New Alchemists were recurring visitors to troubleshoot and monitor the systems. John Todd explained the Ark to filmmakers and journalists. Celebratory stories about the Ark appeared in newspapers, magazines, films, and television in all parts of the world, including French and Japanese national television. And the stories drew thousands of individuals: tourists and locals, government officials and counterculture activists, the enthusiastic and the sceptical. Young people with backpacks were a common sight, hitchhiking east along Highway 2 in the summer months seeking knowledge and inspiration.[37] Though the Ark's life was short (it survived just three years in its intended form), the ripples from these many pilgrimages to Spry Point spread across the planet for decades, bearing witness to the Ark's vision of a beautiful and meaningful life lived in collaboration with nature.

1.30a

1.30b

1.30c

1.30a "Instamatic" photographs of the Ark's opening taken by David Bergmark's parents. Waiting for the helicopters.
1.30b Prime Minister Trudeau mingles with the crowd.
1.30c Prime Minister Trudeau delivering his dedication speech.

2.01

New Alchemy:
Appropriate Technology for Canada's Future

2

Building the Ark for Prince Edward Island was an expression of rising environmental consciousness through the 1970s. Environmentalism emerged from the counterculture – the protest movements resisting the Cold War nuclear arms race, the Vietnam War draft, and the development of nuclear power, as well as the idealism of the civil rights movement and the youth movements of the 1960s. International pro-environmental activism led to the declaration by the United Nations of the first "Earth Day" in 1970. In parallel, a strand of activist, systems-oriented science was challenging the usefulness of traditional reductionist analyses, with the emerging discipline of "ecology" providing scientific rigour to bolster environmental concerns. Finally, with the energy crisis of the mid-1970s, governments began to place serious attention on environmental policy, demonstration projects, and funding. In Canada, activism and geopolitics led to important shifts in federal government attitudes and policies towards the environment. On Prince Edward Island, the provincial government envisioned the island as a test-bed and demonstration site for alternative pathways to development, and offered a venue for the creative collaboration between official culture, local cultures, and the counterculture that would result in the Ark.[1]

Environmental Consciousness: The Emergence of Ecology

Earth Day was first celebrated in April 1970, a symbol of an international grassroots environmental consciousness. It built upon a steadily increasing body of literature, advocacy, and action addressing the many challenges to the environmental integrity of the planet. Earth Day also marked the widespread emergence of the concept of "ecology." In contrast to the approaches of traditional sciences such as biology, geology and chemistry, which study the world by isolation, segregation, and reduction of systems to their simplest components, ecology seeks to understand nature through examining

2.01 New Alchemists on the Sailwing windmill, New Alchemy, Cape Cod, MA, 1977. Sailwing was designed to produce mechanical pumping power to aerate aquaculture tanks, not to produce electricity.

the interconnections of elements within systems. It also carries an overarching view of the Earth's environment as an integrated whole. Rachel Carson's *Silent Spring* brought ecological thinking and the importance of whole system effects of pesticides to millions of readers.[2] "Ecology" and "ecosystem" soon became common terms. Ecological thinking led to a popularization of the notion of "biosphere," defined as the "integrated living and life-support systems comprising the peripheral envelope of the planet Earth," including the natural extent of life forms in its atmosphere and soils.[3] Biosphere awareness and ecological systems thinking were fundamental to the work of the New Alchemists.

Colour photos from the US space program helped to spur this shift in human perception, showing the Earth as singular, finite, and mostly blue and white, a striking contrast to our everyday human experience of an expansive green and brown natural environment. *Whole Earth Catalog* compiler Stewart Brand agitated for the release of these photos, arguing that a picture of the "whole Earth" would fundamentally change human treatment of the planet's environment.[4] The blue and white of oceans and clouds reinforced the "living" nature of the Earth's skin, while the clarity of the edges of the spherical planet underscored the emerging concept of the Earth as having "limits," visually reinforcing the message of Paul Ehrlich's bestselling *The Population Bomb* (1968) and the Club of Rome's *Limits to Growth* (1972), which sold 12 million copies in 37 languages.[5]

The 1968 UNESCO Biosphere Conference in Paris and the 1972 UN Conference on the Human Environment in Stockholm brought these ideas to international policy, eventually leading to the UN World Population Conference of 1974, the Brundtland Report on sustainable development of 1987, the 1992 Rio Earth Summit, and the work of the Intergovernmental Panel on Climate Change today. Canadian diplomat Maurice Strong chaired the Stockholm conference, served from 1972-75 as the first head of the UN Environmental Program (UNEP), and then chaired the Rio Earth Summit of 1992.[6] Canada matched its early international profile on the environment at home, creating the federal agency Environment Canada in 1971, and its Advanced Concepts Centre in 1973 to explore alternative approaches to energy, waste, and policy.

2.02 "Earthrise, December 24, 1968," photographed by Apollo 8 astronaut Bill Anders, who remarked that "we came all this way to explore the moon, and … discovered the earth." The "whole earth" image enhanced the late 1960s rise in environmental consciousness.

Canada's National Energy Policy

The opening of the Ark in 1976 came at the end of a third successive summer of gasoline rationing in Canada and the United States, which refreshed public concerns about energy. The "OPEC Oil Crisis" began in October 1973, when the 11 countries of the Organization of Petroleum Exporting Countries embargoed oil exports to Canada, the USA, western Europe, and other supporters of Israel following the Yom Kippur war. Oil prices rose steeply, while strategic reductions in oil exports at periods of peak demand, such as the winter heating season or the summer travel season, created a powerful climate of insecurity for consumers, and vividly demonstrated Western society's dependence on oil. In contrast, the Ark promised a green, sunny idyll of self-reliance.

Canada's response to the oil crisis included efforts to reduce the impact of energy price changes, programs to develop a more robust array of domestic energy sources (such as fossil fuels, nuclear power, and renewable energy), and a remarkable effort to reorient Canadian society away from consumerism and towards a "Conserver Society." In 1973, Prime Minister Trudeau called for voluntary energy conservation with an appeal to global justice, noting that North Americans constituted 8% of the global population but consumed 38% of the world's energy. For Trudeau, such squandering of resources was not a privilege of the Canadian way of life "but a threat to it."[7] This was followed by a series of short-term policies to balance regional interests by subsidizing eastern Canadian oil imports with a tax on western Canadian exports, and the creation of a national oil company, Petro-Canada, to sell oil at a low cost that would rise steadily towards the world price.[8]

Canada's Ministry of Energy, Mines and Resources was given the task of developing longer-term policies. Its Office of Energy Conservation was established in 1973 and, led by David Brooks, was heavily influenced by E.F. Schumacher's book *Small is Beautiful* (1973), which argued for government economists to cease considering natural resources as expendable income and instead treat non-renewable resources as capital assets. Schumacher's attention to what he saw as the fallacy of unlimited growth, and his arguments in favour of localizing production and consumption in the service of a sufficiency-oriented economy, had a powerful effect on Canadian civil servants, who came "to see their own work as tied to much broader questions about the purpose and structure of human society."[9]

Ecology into Action: Canada as a Conserver Society

Even before the OPEC embargo precipitated an energy crisis in Canada, the Science Council of Canada was preparing a path towards the Conserver Society goal. The Science Council was established in 1966 as an arm's-length agency with a mandate to increase the contribution of science to Canadian society and to provide policy advice based on science and technology.[10] Trudeau increased its funding and valued its advice, believing that its contributions to rational, evidence-based policymaking would be more

2.03 "Bird's eye view of an average gas station in Portland during the early morning hours of pumping when gas was limited on a first-come, first served basis to five gallons per auto." From a series documenting the oil crisis for the US Environmental Protection Agency by photographer David Falconer, December 1973. Similar scenes recurred across the United States and Canada until 1978.

2.04

accountable and (debatably) less politicized. The notion of a Conserver Society was introduced as a secondary element in a 1973 Science Council report on natural resource policy, calling for Canada to "begin the transition from a consumer society preoccupied with resource exploitation to a conserver society engaged in more constructive endeavours."[11] The Conserver Society catchphrase was adopted in the media and within government as the OPEC crisis unfolded, and was widely accepted by the public. In contrast to the predominantly oppositional rhetoric of 1970s environmentalism's "no-growth" and "anti-pollution" messages, the Conserver Society concept was voluntary and activist in tone, and offered a positive vision of a collectively-achieved future.[12] Responding to popular interest, the Council developed a full-blown national strategy in a 1977 report, *Canada as a Conserver Society*, with ground prepared since October 1975 in regular *Conserver Society Notes* newsletters and briefing notes.

University of Toronto metallurgist Ursula Franklin led the Conserver Society report team and drew upon the emerging critique of growth economics posited by E.F. Schumacher and his fellow "sufficiency" economist Kenneth Boulding.[13] "Conserver Society" publications criticized Canada's prevailing resource extraction-based, growth-oriented, industrial technology-obsessed society, proposing instead an alternative future of renewable energy and localized production. To appeal to more traditional ideas of economic development, it also posited a strong export market for Canadian renewable energy technology in the wake of the oil crisis. *Conserver Society Notes* brought the concepts to a household scale in phrases such as "doing more with less" and "re-use, recycling, and … reduction at source."[14] Conserver Society ideas became pervasive in energy and economic policy debate: the New Alchemists framed the Ark in Conserver Society terms, and Prince Edward Island invoked the Conserver Society in seeking federal support for its ambitious 1970s alternative energy projects.

Providing Expertise: The Appropriate Technology Movement

When the promise of the Conserver Society, combined with the menace of the oil crisis, prompted mainstream and government interest in alternative food and energy systems, it quickly became apparent that the requisite expertise would not be found in universities and research institutes. Instead, official culture found itself entering into liberating and sometimes challenging partnerships with counterculture groups such as the New Alchemists. At the opening of the Ark, Stewart Brand queried Trudeau about how his government was able to support such an experimental project as the Ark.

Said Trudeau, 'I have no problem finding money for this sort of project. The problem is finding people to use it well.' He nodded at the Ark. 'How many

2.04 The Conserver Society concept was influential in late 1970s Canadian policy and popular culture. The concept was suggested in the Science Council of Canada Report No. 19 of January 1973, and fully fleshed out in Report No. 27 of September 1977.

groups do you know who could do that?' I was shocked at the question and my
answer – 'Uh. Maybe four, maybe five groups.' He went on, 'I should ask you,
where are the people with the skills going to come from?'[15]

Trudeau recognized the need, even the urgency, to look beyond the usual sources
of policy and practices in the face of an unprecedented energy and environmental
challenge.

The "four, maybe five groups" Brand mentioned might have included such like-
minded contemporaries as Schumacher's own Intermediate Technology Development
Group in London, England; the Centre for Alternative Technology in Machynlleth,
Wales; the Farallones Institute in Berkeley, California; the Biotechnical Research and
Development Institute in the United Kingdom; and McGill University's Minimum Cost
Housing Group in Montreal.[16] All shared a focus on the "how" of exploring alternatives
in action, working on integrated bio-technical systems in a conceptual framework that
the New Alchemists called Appropriate Technology (AT). AT was rooted in Schumacher's
Small is Beautiful proposal of an Intermediate Technology (IT) that would assist
developing countries to achieve social development without going down the road of
global capital and debt. Intermediate Technology regarded goods not as the principal
goal of economic activity, but rather as a byproduct of making people productive.
IT advocated low-cost, accessible technologies, which were best suited to small-
scale applications and compatible with the need for creativity in work. IT contended
that humanity's need is not merely to survive, but to thrive by doing satisfying work
in support of a community. In the 1970s, the Intermediate Technology concept was
adapted to suit conditions in developed countries (including Canada and the USA) and
renamed Alternative Technology (or, as preferred by the New Alchemists, Appropriate
Technology).

Appropriate Technology offered a way out of the displacement, alienation, job losses,
and globalization that seemed to inevitably go hand-in-hand with the most advanced
technologies. Not intended as a romantic or Luddite reaction to high technology, nor
a turning back of the clock, AT sought a broader analysis of the impacts and effects
of technologies, especially their human and societal implications. While "modern"
in seeing technology as a means to advance society, AT insisted that technology be
governed by a social vision, and argued that the highest, most advanced technologies
are often not the best solution. Its proponents anticipated impending societal collapse,
but remained optimistic about the capacity of small social groups to effect meaningful
change. While AT came to be associated with specific devices and techniques (such as
geodesic domes and windmills), it was at its root a mode of *technology-practice* that

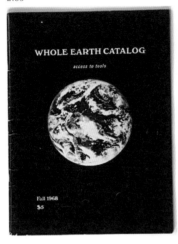

insisted upon a participatory approach to meeting human needs — one that gave equal weight to the technical, socio-political, and ethical implications in making technological choices.[17] AT also recognized the deep unitary basis of technology. Buckminster Fuller and other systems thinkers had pointed out that all energy on planet Earth ultimately comes from one source, the Sun. All energy is solar energy but in different forms: direct solar radiation, convection creating wind to drive windmills, solar evaporation of surface water leading to rainfall and hydro power, and carbohydrates and hydrocarbons from photosynthesis.[18]

A touching aspect of Appropriate Technology literature is the sense of welcome, sharing, and hospitality. The people assembling these pamphlets, posters, and mimeographed pages seemed to really want others to take up the ideas or join them in carrying them out, above all to create a sense of community and common cause. This information exchange has roots in the agricultural improvement pamphlets of the 19th century, and in 20th century magazines such as *Popular Mechanics*, whose articles and back pages were rife with mail-order plans enabling hobbyists to build anything from chicken coops to small airplanes. Comic book back covers and bubble gum packs of the 1960s and 1970s advertised mail-order jokes and gags ("six-foot monster! X-ray specs!") whose improbable technologies and grandiose promises may have helped create a more mature appetite for the enchanting freedoms evoked by a solar oven or geodesic dome in the *Whole Earth Catalog*.[19] The New Alchemists reported receiving up to 100 letters per day seeking information on their projects and systems during 1974.[20]

John Todd referred to *Whole Earth Catalog* compiler Stewart Brand as the Diderot of an emerging world of exploring Appropriate Technology through hands-on action. In the *Catalog*, Brand assembled diverse techniques and examples in a format that emphasized the transmission of technique. The *Catalog* sought to enable individuals to enter into direct, hands-on relationships with technology, which would allow them to do for themselves rather than to be dependent on the decisions of technocratic elites. A reader of the *Whole Earth Catalog* would "find his own inspiration, shape his own environment, and share his adventure with whoever is interested."[21] Through the *Catalog*, the New Alchemists were linked as fellow travellers with groups exploring new possibilities of form, space, lifestyle, and technique, including Ant Farm's inflated transparent pillow structures, Buckminster Fuller's geodesic domes, and Steve Baer's Zomes (non-symmetrical adaptations of geodesic domes, using scavenged automobile roofs). A common quality of these proposals was their focus on the "how" of building — building as a verb – rather than the formal and material outcome of the process – building as object.[22]

2.05 Stewart Brand's first 1968 edition of the *Whole Earth Catalog*. John Todd described Brand as the Diderot of the Appropriate Technology movement.

Appropriate Technology and the New Alchemists partook of what Marshall McLuhan termed the "re-tribalization of society."[23] Re-tribalization had been underway in youth culture since the 1960s and is usually associated with hippie communes and back-to-the-land settlements. McLuhan noted that this movement arose from the realization that knowledge alone is incapable of making change in the world — it must be mobilized and tested through action and experience, to re-enchant the material world as a place of learning. The efforts by the New Alchemists and their allies to directly engage technologies in place constitute a similar re-enchantment of the world and of technology, through that direct experience. While the Appropriate Technology approach is more scientific, focused, and orderly, it shares the mid-1960s "community anarchist" spirit of the Diggers' exhortation to go and "Stake out a retreat. Learn berries and nuts and fruits and small animals and all the plants. Learn water."[24]

At the opening of the Ark, Stewart Brand commented that "the Prime Minister spoke with far more than ceremonial perception,"[25] and it is clear that Trudeau had mastered the underpinnings of the Appropriate Technology movement in preparation for the day. His remarks closed with a critique of society's failure to yet develop a philosophy of machines, which, he argued, is needed to turn techniques into a meaningful technology. Trudeau's understanding of "technology" followed the ideas of "Conserver Society" advocate Ursula Franklin who, in her later Massey Lectures "The Real World of Technology," followed Jacques Ellul in seeing technology not as gadgets and devices, but as "the way things are done around here," a conception that encompasses the tool, the user, and their social milieu.[26] Appropriate Technology practitioners, Conserver Society proponents, and New Alchemists all drew upon Schumacher's ideas about technology and its potential as a source of either individual alienation or creative fulfillment, depending on its scale and control. By the end of the 1970s, the Appropriate Technology movement reached its zenith, with the Ark and similar demonstrations funded by the Canadian government, the popular acceptance of the notion of "Canada as a conserver society," and even President Jimmy Carter installing solar panels on the White House roof and speaking of the "adventure" of alternative energy.

The New Alchemists: "flexible lifestyles" and "hard science"
Drawing on the motivations and practices of the Appropriate Technology movement, the New Alchemists sought to reconcile technology with culture in pursuit of a healthy future, liberated from consumerism and the environmental threats posed by fossil fuels and nuclear energy. John Todd, a Canadian-born marine biologist, and Bill McLarney, an ichthyologist, met as graduate students at the University of Michigan in the late

2.06

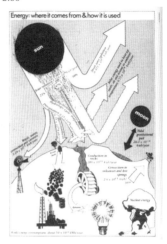

2.06 "Energy: where it comes from and how it is used," Peter Harper and Godfey Boyle, *Radical Technology*, 1976, 57. This diagram is a reminder that all available energy on the planet (with the arguable exception of nuclear fission) is a form of solar energy.

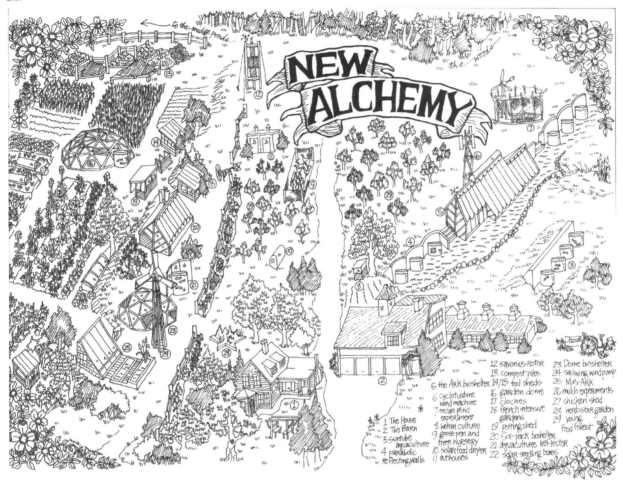

1. The House
2. The Barn
3. Suntube aquaculture
4. parabolic reflecting walls
5. the ARK bioshelter
6. cycloturbine wind machine
7. solar pond experiment
8. worm culture
9. goose pen and tree nursery
10. solar food dryer
11. outhouses
12. savonius rotor
13. compost piles
14/15. tool sheds
16. garden dome
17. cloches
18. french intensive gardens
19. potting shed
20. six-pack bioshelter
21. aquaculture reflector
22. solar seedling boxes
23. Dome bioshelter
24. sailwing windpump
25. Mini-ARK
26. mulch experiments
27. chicken shed
28. herb-star garden
29. young food forest

2.07 "New Alchemy" site map by Maia Massion, *The Journal of the New Alchemists* 5, 1979, 7. New Alchemy's Cape Cod MA farm and research centre was an eclectic assembly of improvised structures and experiments in aquaculture, agriculture, and renewable energy.

1960s (where Todd studied under the pioneering ecologist Marston Bates), and later both took positions at San Diego State College.[27] Together with Todd's wife Nancy Jack Todd, they were dismayed by the "unremitting flow of information about the destruction of the environment."[28] In 1971, they set up on a rented farm on Cape Cod to explore ecological alternatives to the prevailing destructive methods of sustaining humanity, beginning with alternative food and energy systems – organic agriculture and land-based aquaculture. Their name was meant to hark back to a time when science, art, and philosophy were not mutually exclusive realms of knowledge.[29] For Todd "the interfaces between science, politics and society were of legitimate concern for scientists. ... We felt it imperative to fuse science with the practical, scholarly and philosophic realms."[30] Their influences included Schumacher and Brand, the ecological modelling work of Howard T. Odum, poet Wendell Berry's reflections on locally-appropriate polyculture farming, and anthropologist Margaret Mead's arguments for community-level social change leadership. New Alchemy's motto, reproduced on their letterhead and all publications through the 1970s, proclaimed no small ambition: "To restore the lands, protect the seas, and inform the earth's stewards," and was guided by seven principles:

1. People must participate in the processes that sustain them; people and process must be one.
2. Subcomponents of life – food, energy, shelter, manufacture – must be reintegrated at the point of end use.
3. Scale of systems (physical and political) must be reduced to be truly participatory.
4. Technology and systems must be tuned to the bioregion; seek local rather than universal solutions.
5. Human needs must be fused with the needs of the biosphere; ecosystems must be enhanced by human presence.
6. Inexhaustible energy sources – sun, wind, biofuels – must be the primary inputs.
7. Living, organic processes must be substituted for energy consuming and polluting processes.[31]

On Cape Cod, the New Alchemists attracted a group of like-minded people who helped out, the more committed being drawn into the community.[32] The nearby Woods Hole Oceanographic Institution provided salaried employment for Todd and McLarney, which sustained the Institute's work and provided a milieu sympathetic to experiential research. While many New Alchemists possessed advanced degrees, they did not regard expertise as a refuge for unchallenged authority. Traditional scientific publication was seen as an impediment to direct action; the urgent priority was to evaluate relevant knowledge through direct experimentation, and to directly disseminate the results to people who would put it into practice in the real world.[33] Adapting the spirit of the original alchemists of early modern science who sought to use their special knowledge to transmute base materials into gold, the New Alchemists sought to infuse the creative power of nature with the controlling potential of technology in order to liberate human culture. Reconciling technology with the humanities, and science with culture, "the new alchemy" would transform people from consumerist spectators to participating producers, with agency in their own lives.[34]

2.08

2.09

2.08 Saturday afternoon at New Alchemy, 1977. John Todd holds court at the left foreground. Saturdays were visiting days, starting with a morning work party, followed by a potluck lunch. Afternoons were tours, presentations, and informal seminars such as this.
2.09 Gardening at New Alchemy with a geodesic dome greenhouse in the background, 1977.

2.10

While John Todd provided a visionary sense of direction, research priorities were established by consensus through (often lengthy) community meetings. Individuals were also permitted to opt into projects of personal interest and to cajole others to assist. The organizational hierarchy was flat and everyone was paid the same salary. Donations from individual supporters augmented contributions to the budget from a relatively small number of grants; the pursuit of a "new paradigm" did not fit well into most granting mandates. The Rockefeller Brothers Foundation was a recurring supporter and Stewart Brand's Point Foundation provided a key grant in 1974, but for the most part, New Alchemy's cash needs in this period were met by the founders' Woods Hole salaries, augmented by an increasing number of individual member-supporters from around the world.[35]

Like many in the Appropriate Technology movement, the New Alchemists shared the scope and practice of their wholesome integration of work and life through a publication. Seven volumes of the *Journal of the New Alchemists* appeared between 1973 and 1981, edited by Nancy Jack Todd; a selection of articles was republished in *Book of the New Alchemists* (1977).[36] The *Journal* set an intimate tone through photographs of community activities: pot luck meals and celebrations, work in the

2.11

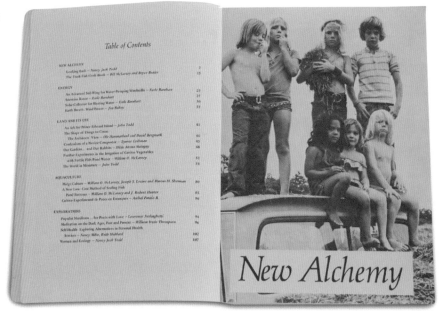

2.10 Covers of *The Journal of the New Alchemists* 2 (1974) and 4 (1977). The high production values and mix of intimate and scientific content made the *Journal* a popular success.
2.11 Interior page spread from *Journal* 3, 1976. The children attest to New Alchemy's interest in research integrated with everyday life, and their commitment to a liberated future.

gardens, fishponds, or raising a wind turbine pole. Photographs show gatherings of hippie-looking folk with long hair and beards, beads on bare chests, bikini tops and long skirts and short shorts, and beautiful young children taking part in everything. These images, along with the *Journal*'s bio-psychedelic titles and borders and the intimate stream-of-consciousness articles on the life and times of the New Alchemists, led many to presume they were a back-to-the-land commune. John Todd's somewhat mystical-poetic speculations about the future of human society and the role of the work of the New Alchemists added to the publication's charisma. Stewart Brand observed that "everything in the press has been about the New Alchemists rather than by them, and usually, the emphasis has been on their flexible lifestyle rather than their hard science."[37] But equally prominent in the *Journal* were scientific reports on the various projects in food production, energy generation, and integration of systems, complete with clear diagrams of system designs, accounts of operation, and rigorous data collection and analysis. The sumptuous production values of the *Journal*, which was printed on high-quality paper and professionally typeset and bound, stand in stark contrast to the underground quality of related Alternate Technology publications such as Steve Baer's *Dome Cookbook*, Boyle and Harper's *Radical Technology*, and even Brand's *Whole Earth Catalog*. The *Journal* provided a vivid picture of a life in a purposeful community, along with useful information for fellow-travellers of all sorts. It showed that the New Alchemy community stretched far beyond the farmstead; in 1978 there were 2,500 dues-paying supporters around the world.[38] As well as the *Journal*, New Alchemy offered an extensive list of reports, publications, and plans by mail order.

Within a few years, the New Alchemy community extended further still, thanks to the *Journal*, the 1974 National Film Board of Canada film *The New Alchemists*,[39] and a steady flow of positive newspaper and magazine stories. John Hess, food critic for the New York *Times*, visited New Alchemy to sample their first harvest of farmed tilapia. His published review declared, "It's good – it really is good!"[40] With news coverage, the unusual farm-based research institute became an attraction for the sympathetic and the curious, to the point that drop-in visitors became an impediment to their work. Saturdays were designated as open farm days. Visitors and New Alchemists worked together on projects around the farm until noon, followed by a communal meal of food from the gardens and potluck dishes on the lawn. Lectures, tours, and informal conversations would extend into the afternoon. Among the visitors were Nobel Peace Prize recipient George Wald and astronaut Rusty Schweikart.[41] Others who never visited the farm nonetheless felt a part of the community, and membership dues flowed in from around the globe.

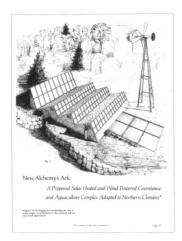

2.12

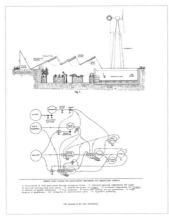

The Advent of the New Alchemy Ark Concept

New Alchemy's Ark originated not in building, but in biology. Their Cape Cod Alchemy Farm experiments focused on food systems: organic agriculture, intensive deep-soil greenhouse agriculture, and land-based aquaculture systems providing low-energy protein. Enclosures were improvised to mitigate the environmental conditions, with parallel efforts to develop energy sources to pump the water, generate electricity, and heat air and water. It was a diverse catalogue of approaches, yielding a large body of observational data, but architecturally it was incoherent, a mixed bag of semi-vernacular shed roofs and shingle boxes, geodesic domes, and improvised insulated shutters, scattered across the landscape accompanied by a Rube Goldberg-style gadgetry of windmills and solar panels. The crazy-quilt randomness of Alchemy Farm fostered a sense of magical possibility – a feeling that any idea might lead to just about any possible outcome – like the unexpected gadgets that were always just around the next corner on the farm.

Nancy Willis worked on organic agriculture at New Alchemy starting in 1973. In 1974, she brought her neighbour David Bergmark, a recent architecture graduate, to the Cape Cod farm. Bergmark described his first visit to the site in near-mystical terms:

> There was a full moon, there were sailwing windmills, there were solar collectors, there was trickling water, the whole experience was an experience of sound and sight. I was awestruck because … I'd read quite a bit about alternative technologies, but I really hadn't seen a group of people who were … really understanding how they worked together.[42]

By late 1973, the successes of the New Alchemists' agriculture and aquaculture system experiments led to proposals to integrate these into a single designed ecosystem: a glass-covered aquaculture pond heated by a solar panel and direct sunlight, and a sunken greenhouse drawing heat from the pond and from a geothermal loop; the prominent windmill provided energy for the pumps.[43] Aquaculture would yield several crops of tilapia in summer and a single crop of trout and perch in winter, providing enough cash return to finance the construction and maintenance costs. Greenhouse agriculture would produce high value vegetables and greens, fertilized by the fish waste, providing additional income. Ecologist Earle Barnhart, a recent arrival to New Alchemy, provided crucial systems design skills to the project team; he also coined the name "Ark" to express the hope for renewal symbolized by the design. Once coined, the name "Ark" stuck, and the New Alchemists' own understanding of their work adjusted to suit the name. According to John Todd:

> By using the outrageous term Ark, we meant [to include] representative examples

of all the great kingdoms of life on the planet: the bacteria, and the fungi, and the protozoa, and the algae, and the plants, and the woody plants, the trees and the shrubs, and the mollusks and the snails and the fish and the people, and we really meant it.[44]

In 1974, a Mini-Ark was built on the Cape Cod farm, putting the synthesis of this proposal into testable action, and launching the Ark concept into the world through the *Journal* and other media. For hundreds of thousands of readers of lavishly illustrated stories in *Smithsonian* magazine and *Canadian Weekend Magazine* (among many others), the Mini-Ark provided photographic evidence of the imminent arrival of an alternative future.[45]

Like the biblical Noah, the New Alchemists acted with a sense of hope in the face of impending doom. John Todd continually referred to a coming apocalypse that might include nuclear war or meltdown, economic collapse, and/or societal breakdown due to population growth and food shortages. In January 1975, he sent a "survival blueprint for Prince Edward Island" to PEI government advisor Andy Wells for the provincial government's attention and action, writing in his cover letter "yes, I am quite serious about it all [the impending collapse], and feel we must consider the island itself as an ark."[46] Todd's eschatology was in line with that of many other thinkers and commentators, on a spectrum from the counterculture to United Nations officials, all questioning the sustainability of human systems on earth. At the same time, Todd was able to spin poetic images of renewed, healthy, and fulfilling human communities living in collaboration with nature. This curious mix of apocalyptic and Edenic thinking was shared by many counterculture and environmental groups, whose rhetoric embraced the imminent destruction or collapse of society but also visions of a wholesome and meaningful lifestyle that embraced different goals. Their Ark ambitions were global, and the New Alchemists sought to test the concept and systems in a variety of climates and settings. Bill McLarney established a tropical outpost in Costa Rica in 1973.[47] According to Nancy Todd, the Canadian Maritimes had a magnetic pull for John Todd as a northern climate opportunity.[48] Each of the Arks that ensued would contain the biology and ecology needed to support a new and improved vision of human society.

The New Alchemists Come to Prince Edward Island

Millions of Canadians encountered the sunny vision of New Alchemy as a relief from the depths of the first winter of the oil crisis. In February 1974, *The Canadian Magazine*, a national weekend newspaper supplement, published "The World That Feeds Itself," a celebratory account of the New Alchemy Ark as a viable alternative for

2.13 John Todd (right) by the midge pond at New Alchemy, with the Mini-Ark in the background, 1977.

Canada's food and energy future. In a passing comment, John Todd declared an interest in building an Ark on PEI, if grant money could be found.[49] Hundreds of Canadians were inspired to send in membership dues to New Alchemy in the months following the article.[50] Official recognition also followed. Bruce McCallum of Environment Canada's Advanced Concepts Centre was doing research towards their 1974 report *Environmentally Appropriate Technology – Technologies for a Conserver Society*.[51] He visited the New Alchemy farm in summer 1974, and was impressed by their projects and people as important sources of expertise on alternative systems. McCallum was then assembling an informal Ottawa "eco-network" of ecologically-oriented people within federal agencies, including the Science Council, the Office of Energy Conservation, the National Research Council, and the Canada Mortgage and Housing Corporation; Prime Minister Trudeau's personal speechwriter Joy Kogawa also took part.[52] This network would play an important role, both officially and through back channels, in the Ark and many other projects that members hoped would "revolutionize the way humans interact with the biosphere."[53] McCallum presented preliminary video footage from the NFB film *The New Alchemists* to the network, building cross-department Federal enthusiasm for their work. He also informed John Todd of early plans for an "Institute for Energy and Environment" on Prince Edward Island, offering the possibility that New Alchemy's interest in the Island might be reciprocated.[54]

Prince Edward Island's provincial government saw the OPEC Oil Crisis and the Conserver Society concept as opportunities to address a longstanding existential challenge, a striking contrast to other provinces that perceived these as threats to their growth-based, consumer-driven prosperity and comfort. Since his election in 1966, Premier Alex Campbell had sought a meaningful way forward for Canada's smallest province in the face of globalization. As the son of a former Premier, raised in Summerside, the Island's second largest city, Campbell was expected to adhere to rural ideals of continuity and tradition. Instead, Campbell's relatively radical interest in alternative pathways of development was signalled as early as 1967 in his famous "I am a Canadian" speech, in which he argued for a focus on regional self-sufficiency in Atlantic Canada, and proposed the Island as a test-bed for locally-oriented development that could model solutions to national challenges, including pollution. By 1973, Campbell had embraced the economic ideas of E.F. Schumacher's book *Small is Beautiful*, including a focus on regionally-oriented development and the acceptance of limits to growth.[55]

The 1973 OPEC embargo had severe effects on an island which had neither conventional energy resources nor a trunk electrical connection to the mainland; all electricity was generated using imported oil. Yet Campbell echoed Schumacher

2.14 "The World That Feeds Itself," *The Canadian Magazine*, February 9, 1974, 2-3. This article led hundreds of Canadians to send membership dues to New Alchemy, and inspired provincial and federal officials to support John Todd's idea for a northern bioshelter demonstration.

2.14

in arguing against national oil price subsidies, seeing them as a disincentive to conservation and renewables. Speaking at a meeting of Canadian provincial premiers, Campbell said,

> What I am presenting to you then, is a suggestion, not for a new society, but for a new direction to our society. One that emphasizes self-reliance and involvement of our citizens rather than encouraging them to be passive consumers. … I am one who believes that small is not only beautiful but in the long run, more practicable.[56]

Amory Lovins' concept of "soft energy paths" – small, local, diverse, and renewable sources – over "hard energy paths" – large, centralized, capital intensive, and non-renewable – also resonated with Campbell.[57]

In an analysis developed with his advisor Andy Wells, Campbell argued that mainstream development (based on centralization, rationalization, and consolidation) offered only bleak prospects for a small, isolated island province. Continued industrialization and globalization would render PEI increasingly marginal in the world economy; instead, PEI needed a different form of progress that would offer a meaningful future for Islanders.[58] Wells' interest in environmental causes and renewable energy, and his opposition to nuclear power, provided an ecological orientation for advancing this vision. Wells began to build a network of contacts and collaborators, which quickly overlapped McCallum's Ottawa-based network. Wells and Campbell both attended "The Uses of Smallness" conference in Rensselaer, NY (1974), where they mooted their plans for an energy and environment institute on PEI.[59]

Federal and Island interest in alternative approaches converged in Fall 1974, when Bruce McCallum invited John Todd to Ottawa as the main presenter for a "Conserver Society" workshop. McCallum's boss Robert Durie called Todd's presentations "striking demonstrations of the relevance of your program to several long range issues that are the concern of [Environment Canada]: food shortages, declining energy reserves, ecological stability, man's impact on global climate, resource carrying capacity, … and so on."[60] There, Wells made direct contact with John Todd, offered an Island site for a demonstration Ark, and introduced him to Lynne Douglas of the federal Ministry of State for Urban Affairs (MSUA).[61]

MSUA was leading preparations for Habitat '76, the United Nations Conference on Human Settlements, to be held in Vancouver as a follow-up to the 1972 Stockholm Conference. Habitat '76 intended to focus the general global concern for the state of the planet on specific measures and actions related to human settlements. To support this, MSUA ran the Urban Demonstration Program, a national competition to showcase demonstration projects (not necessarily urban as it turned out) across the country, to

2.15

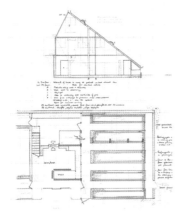

2.16

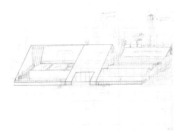

2.15 Ark for PEI Habitat '76 Design, plan, and sections, scale 1 inch = 8 feet. Drawing by Earle Barnhart & Hilde Maingay, pencil and ink on graph paper, November 1974. Informed by the then-limited literature on solar energy and greenhouse agriculture, Barnhart and Maingay pieced together an assembly of systems in guise of a building.
2.16 Ark for PEI Habitat '76 Design, perspective view. Drawing by Earle Barnhart & Hilde Maingay, pencil and ink on graph paper, November 1974. While this view closely anticipates the final presentation drawing, it also demonstrates the limited visualization skills held by the New Alchemists.

show Canada's leadership and action as host nation.[62] It was Douglas' job to solicit, vet, and promote proposals under this program, bound by the guidelines that projects should be both innovative and based on proven technology. The latter requirement necessitated some creative rationalization in defending the Ark proposal. Robert Durie was also enthusiastic about an Ark on PEI as a way of testing New Alchemy concepts in a northern climate, and encouraged the group to use Habitat '76 as a vehicle for these ambitions. He also committed Advanced Concepts Centre funds and technical support for Ark design development over and above any Urban Demonstration grant received. Here was the potential grant money John Todd had wished for in *The Canadian Magazine*. Careful coaching from the provincial and federal officials helped the New Alchemists prepare a compelling proposal for the competition, submitted in November 1974.

Andy Wells set about fulfilling the Island government's offer of a suitable site, eventually offering land at Spry Point, an hour east of Charlottetown on the coast. The reasons for choosing Spry Point for the Ark's landing place were never laid out in articles on the Ark, nor communicated to provincial officials. Tom Connors, then provincial Deputy Minister of Development, thought that its remoteness was intended to emphasize the Ark's goal of self-sufficiency.[63] John Todd stated recently that "I wanted the site to be remote. My dream was a whole eco-technic village. I visited with Andy Wells and [Lynne Douglas] and fell in love with the [Spry Point] site."[64] A back-to-the-Island counterculture community was already established at nearby Wood Islands, but there would be little interaction with New Alchemy. Pre-existing plans for a tourist beach and nature park on the site were deemed compatible by the New Alchemists and provincial officials: "The public would be given the opportunity for recreation and would also be given an insight into what the scope of the New Alchemy Project would be all about."[65] In addition to its instructive value as a demonstration, the Ark could have significant tourism potential to introduce beach visitors to new ideas about living.

An Ark for Prince Edward Island:
New Alchemy's Habitat '76 Competition Design

New Alchemy's November 1974 submission to the Urban Demonstration competition comprised nearly 50 pages of background discussion and detailed description.[66] The design challenge was significantly more complex than anything yet encountered. Scaling up the Ark concept to create a self-sufficient bioshelter in a hostile northern climate marked a new level of ambition to integrate individual systems into a complex enhanced ecosystem. Diligent work with graph paper and pencils by New Alchemists

Earle Barnhart and Hilde Maingay assembled the New Alchemy puzzle pieces of greenhouse agriculture, aquaculture, and building ecology.[67] Reference sources were scarce. Barnhart's notes on the design principles drew upon Victor Olgyay's *Design with Climate* for issues of site planning and building form, and Bruce Anderson's *Solar Energy and Shelter Design* for basic solar system design and performance. Elvin McDonald's *Handbook for Greenhouse Gardeners* provided well-tested conventional guidelines, while an article by Javed Maghsood provided early information on a solar greenhouse design under development at McGill University's Brace Research Institute.[68] This first "Ark for Prince Edward Island" design was three storeys tall on the south face, tucked into the ground on the north, with two windmill towers and a sheltering hedgerow to the north. The central dwelling and labs zone was clad in wood shingles, cut away at each level for balconies or entry, and flanked by a stone chimney. A matching wedge of glass to the west contained four rectangular concrete fishponds, with two ranks of sloped solar collector panels above the tanks. A low sawtooth-roofed greenhouse containing raised planting beds was to the east.

This early concept for the PEI Ark gave a significant portion of the building's south face to a blank surface of shingles. Aquaculture and agriculture were segregated in two wings, and the aquaculture greenhouse was a huge volume enclosed by a vast surface of glass which would be difficult to heat in the winter season. Its solar panels used water trickling over dark metal to collect heat, which was expected to come from the air as well as from direct solar impact. The agricultural greenhouse was segregated to manage overheating in the afternoon sun; the potential of balancing energy needs by combining aquaculture and agriculture in a single space was not yet recognized. A Clivus Multrum composting system fed human wastes back into the nutrient cycle.

The New Alchemists had the capacity to resolve the biology, but achieving architectural coherence was elusive, and the creation of convincing visualizations was beyond their skills. Architect David Bergmark, by now a regular volunteer at the farm, pitched in for several days at the last minute to create professional-quality plans and sections of the Ark based on Barnhart's graph paper sketches, adding significant credibility to the building proposal. Certainly the most important of Bergmark's drawings, and arguably the most important element of the proposal as a whole, was the dreamscape of the future that graced the cover: the perspective drawing of a futuristic glass building set in a rural idyll of hedgerows and ploughed fields (2.20).

"An Ark for Prince Edward Island" was the lead project in the press release announcing the Urban Demonstration Program competition winners in April 1975, and the New Alchemy Institute received $354,000 for research, design, development, and

2.17

2.18

2.17 "Section AA and Section BB, An Ark of New Alchemy," Ark for PEI Habitat '76 Design, scale 1 inch = 8 feet. Design by Earle Barnhart & Hilde Maingay, drawing by David Bergmark, ink on tracing paper, November 1974. Recent graduate architect David Bergmark provided a few days of assistance to make professional drawings of the Barnhart and Maingay Ark design.

2.18 "Plan, An Ark of New Alchemy," Ark for PEI Habitat '76 Design, scale 1 inch = 8 feet. Design by Earle Barnhart & Hilde Maingay, drawing by David Bergmark, ink on tracing paper, November 1974. Bergmark's drawings were essential to the New Alchemy Institute proposal to the Urban Demonstration Program funding competition for Habitat '76.

construction.[69] Many of the published news stories featured a drawing of the Ark; the coverage was intense and positive, on the Island and beyond. The New Alchemy Institute – Prince Edward Island collaboration became a beacon of possibility for an alternative, ecological approach to living. Both Premier Alex Campbell and John Todd perceived the Island as well prepared to receive the gifts of the Ark and to share them with the world. Campbell saw the Ark as a return to more authentic principles:

> There was a time in years past when Prince Edward Island could virtually supply all of its needs. Over the years, however, we have come to depend more and more on mainland Canada for the staples of life. Hopefully, the Ark will help to turn us in the right direction again. We still remember the old ways here and we are still a little old fashioned in any case. In a few years, maybe every Island family will be living in its own Ark.[70]

In parallel to the effort to secure Ark funding, Campbell and Wells pushed ahead with their vision of the Island as a world leader in Appropriate Technology and renewable energy. In late 1975, Campbell convinced his cabinet to opt out of an investment in New Brunswick's Point Lepreau Nuclear Generating Station, motivated by his own ambivalence about such a "hard energy path" and influenced by Wells' passionate economic, environmental, and ethical opposition.[71] The province did move ahead with the cable link to New Brunswick; when it was completed in October 1977, Campbell argued that the cable "enabled soft technology" through grid interconnection.[72]

To foster this "soft path" thinking, the province held a four-day Energy Days extravaganza in the spring of 1976. Organized as hearings of the Island legislature, the first two days presented the current state of conventional thinking on energy, setting up the final two days for international thought leaders in the area (including Amory Lovins, George McRobie, and John Todd) to make the closing case for energy alternatives.

Energy Days also set the stage for the emergence of the "Institute for Man and Resources" (IMR). Campbell had announced the creation of IMR in January 1975, fulfilling the proposal developed in summer 1974.[73] IMR remained inactive until Wells was named Director in June 1976, at which point it began "the analysis, invention, adaptation and application of appropriate energy, food and crop production and living and shelter systems which are socially desirable and ecologically sustainable."[74] IMR set six research themes: wood heating, wind energy, solar energy, energy conservation, low-head hydroelectric energy, and community energy systems.[75] Though focused on the Island, it would seek to fulfill the ambition of Campbell's 1969 speech and offer a test-bed for solutions to serve Canada and the world.[76]

2.19 Ark for PEI, model of Habitat '76 design viewed from southwest, scale 1 inch = 8 feet. Model by Lucas McDowell and David Burlock with Megan Peck, ash, basswood and 3D-printed polymer, October 2016.
2.20 "An Ark of New Alchemy," Ark for PEI Habitat '76 Design, Perspective View. Design by Earle Barnhart & Hilde Maingay, drawing by David Bergmark, ink on tracing paper, November 1974. Bergmark's rendering adds a sense of substance to the design, and a suggestive rural Island landscape that helped capture public imagination.

Todd saw the Ark as a tool of regional liberation, suited to its place and capable of being made in its place, which would enable local talent to flourish, rather than being forced into "goin' down the road" to the alienating industrial jobs of Toronto:

> Within the paradigm of working within one's limits, regions like Maritime Canada will begin to flower again, because they will be no longer linked, in a dependency sense, to the technologies of central Canada.[77]

What made the proposed Ark for Prince Edward Island distinct from previous New Alchemy constructions was its human dimension. For the first time, the enclosure was imagined as an environment for sustained human habitation. The Ark marked the culmination of the individual food system studies, inaugurating a new orientation towards systems synthesis and the active integration of building design. Much specific development remained to be carried out, yet the core concepts of the Ark were already present: a strong distinction between the north and south sides (recognizing that at the Island latitude, available solar energy is more than double on the south side); the use of earth banks and trees to provide a sheltered microclimate; and the integration of solar and wind energy systems with biological systems. To move the ideas forward into a true synthesis, architecture would need to play a more integrated and collaborative role with biology.

2.20

AN ARK

maingay barnhart

①F NEW ALCHEMY

Solsearch Architects:
Designing an Ecological Architecture

3

A dreamscape of an ecological future appeared in countless newspapers and magazines across Canada in early summer of 1975. This was David Bergmark's drawing of "An Ark for Prince Edward Island," accompanying publication of the Urban Demonstration Program competition results.[1] The Ark was by far the most visionary of the ten winners, and since it offered the richest story, it was often the most fully described. While New Alchemy's "family-sized food, energy and housing complex" provided a convincing image for the public and the Habitat '76 officials, much hard work and an entirely new level of technological imagination would be needed to transform the vision into a functioning building. Adding to the challenge, the federal funds and the Province's gift of the Spry Point site came with the expectation that the Ark would be presented at Habitat '76 in Vancouver as a finished project. The Urban Demonstration showcase was to open in October 1976, less than eighteen months from the announcement of funding.

The New Alchemists were given early notice in January 1975 that the Ark project would receive funding, and because of the tight timeframe they began design development in advance of a formal contract. They could rely on their extensive experience with food production systems, both agriculture and aquaculture, but their energy experiments were rudimentary, not much beyond the hopeful examples presented in the *Whole Earth Catalog*, and their building enclosures were even less developed. Early in 1975, David Bergmark joined Earle Barnhart and Hilde Maingay for a trip to Ottawa to review the Habitat '76 Ark design with the Technical Review panel assembled by Environment Canada's Advanced Concepts Centre. The review affirmed the basic concepts of the Ark's biological systems, but expressed significant reservations about the building structure, enclosure, and energy systems. It became clear to the New Alchemists that the technical challenges would require expertise in building design,

3.02

3.01 Solsearch Architects sketching session, Spring 1975. David Bergmark (left) and Ole Hammarlund (right).
3.02 Barbara McAndrew, "PEI chosen for ecological ark plan to perfect self-sufficient living unit," the *Globe and Mail*, 4 July 1975, B1. David Bergmark's drawing was published with many stories about the Urban Demonstration Program competition.

3.03

energy systems, and construction beyond their ken. Over the next twenty months, in close collaboration with two young architects, and eventually supported by builders from the local community on Prince Edward Island, the New Alchemists assembled a community capable of realizing a remarkably mature work of ecological architecture.

New Alchemy and Solsearch:
A New Level of Collaboration, February 1975

Following the challenging technical review, New Alchemy invited David Bergmark to take the lead on architectural design for the Ark. In turn, Bergmark, a recently-graduated architect, partnered with his friend Ole Hammarlund, a registered architect with an established design-build practice in Cambridge, Massachusetts. Hammarlund had qualified as a master carpenter in his native Denmark and studied architecture at the Royal Danish Academy before emigrating to complete his architecture degree at the Massachusetts Institute of Technology. Bergmark had previously worked as a builder, on his own and for Hammarlund. Following a year of architectural study at the University of British Columbia, he transferred to Yale's architecture school, where design-build and self-build projects were prominent. Construction experiences fed the hands-on nature of their design approach, which would prove crucial for the success of the Ark. Over a February 1975 weekend, they cooked up the name "Solsearch Architects" and designed the sun logo and business cards. Together they possessed distinct but complementary skills and personalities. Bergmark's drawings had been crucial to the success of the Habitat '76 proposal; now Hammarlund's eloquent hand brought a sense of life to the next visualizations of the Ark, notably the aerial perspective view that would feature on the poster. The Solsearch collaboration was immersive, with a continuous exchange of ideas through sketching, drawing, models, and discussion; the two architects often worked simultaneously on the same model or study.[2] As a start-up firm, Solsearch had unusual freedom in approaching the Ark.

> Hammarlund: The Ark project was very unusual compared to anything we had done before or after. We had just this one job; no one else was calling us about something else we had to do. We could sit down and concentrate on this for days, we could live it. It was all about this job.
>
> Bergmark: It was not nine to five. It was twenty-four hours a day, seven days a week, calling each other up and saying "Hey, I have an idea for this." We pinched ourselves and asked ourselves if we were working or just having fun.[3]

Solsearch entered into a contract with New Alchemy for the design of the Ark; the architects were formally separate from the Institute, though their relationship was quite close. Solsearch brought design and visualization skills to the collaboration, along with experience of building and construction management. Working closely with the New Alchemists, they worked to bring the various systems together into a coherent and communicative form. The New Alchemists found an architect's ability to visualize space in three dimensions to be a revelation. Nancy Willis recalls realizing that a design sketch "can be incredible, because it kind of puts together all your thoughts. We were so glad to get this expertise that we didn't have. Those drawings by Earle and Hilde were so basic. Sitting around the table when David and Ole started sketching – we were thinking 'Wow! This is where we want to go!'"[4] Earle Barnhart and Hilde Maingay were happy to let the architects run with their Ark concept, which freed them to concentrate on refining the food systems.[5] Solsearch worked to synthesize architecture and biological systems in a coherent and communicative form, paying attention to the quality of the human environment resulting from the science.

Solsearch also brought awareness of current thinking about ecological design within architectural practice. Solar design and building energy were topics increasingly covered in architecture school coursework. Bergmark and Hammarlund built their knowledge by consulting the emerging solar design literature and examples. The Saskatchewan Conservation House, which was being designed at the same time as the PEI Ark, provided one credible and substantial example of integrated energy design.[6] The Solsearch library contained the *Portola Institute Energy Primer* (1974) and *Alternative Sources of Energy: Practical Technology and Philosophy for a Decentralized Society* (1975), along with the ubiquitous *Whole Earth Catalog*. An old copy of the *ASHRAE Fundamentals*, the "bible" for mechanical engineers, provided the basis for an almost continuous exercise of calculating energy needs for the Ark.[7]

Unusually for the era, Solsearch looked beyond the concept of solar energy as a system to be "added" to a building, instead seeking to understand energy flow as a first principle of building form. They worked to determine energy needs and available solar energy in a design situation, and were inspired to conceive of building form in terms of energy harvesting capacity. Cross-sections of early Solsearch designs typically included annotation of the energy harvest potential of building surfaces. But predicting solar energy performance remained a source of grinding anxiety throughout the design process. Bergmark recalls "We had so many questions all the time, about everything, that we would always go out and seek people out to give us some information – 'What do you know about how much heat gain we're going to get through these windows?'" Hammarlund adds "How many collectors do you need? Nobody knew."[8] Meanwhile, even during design, the publicity surrounding the Ark's development led other designers

3.03 Solsearch Architects business cards. Solsearch Architects, two-colour offset lithograph, 1975-76.

3.04

3.05

3.04 New Alchemists and Solsearch Architects visiting Spry Point, February 1975. The trip was a vivid illustration of the harsh winter conditions on the Island, and of the energy potential of sunlight reflected up off the snow-covered ground.
3.05 Spry Point site concept sketch. Drawing by Ole Hammarlund, Solsearch Architects, Ink and Marker on Mylar, Summer 1975. The Ark anchors site development including multiple windmills, a large geodesic dome, and several greenhouses.
3.06 "Lower Level [Plan]," Ark for PEI first Solsearch design, scale 1 inch = 8 feet. Solsearch Architects, pencil and marker on tracing paper, ca. March 1975. Aquaculture is housed in large concrete tanks, and no separate space for a kitchen greenhouse is provided to serve the dwelling.
3.07 "Section," Ark for PEI first Solsearch design, scale 1 inch = 8 feet. Solsearch Architects, pencil and marker on tracing paper, ca. March 1975. This first Solsearch design introduces the concept of the building as an energy collector, with the greenhouse running the full extent of the southern exposure, and a solid volume containing other functions to the north.

to seek out Solsearch for reliable information about solar design.[9]

So it was that two young architects came to design a major building on radically new principles, embodying multiple experimental systems. Nancy Jack Todd introduced Solsearch to readers of the *Journal* as "architecture's answer to New Alchemy."[10] Their limited experience of conventional architectural practice was perhaps an asset; they remained open-minded about the role of architecture in an experimental project, and were willing to engage with much more than the architectural enclosure. Over the next eight months, Solsearch refined the Ark by developing three major versions of the design. In addition to the sketches, drawings and models that are usual in architecture, they designed and built the "Six-Pack," a small test greenhouse, to explore the architecture-biology interactions at full-scale and in real time. And at the last moment, Solsearch stepped up to lead the construction of the Ark on its Spry Point site. At the same time, they worked in parallel to design and build a smaller "Cape Cod Ark" on the New Alchemy farm. Altogether, this was an adventure into uncharted design territory.

First Solsearch Ark Design, March 1975

With Solsearch now leading the architectural design, the PEI Ark design underwent a significant formal and systems evolution. Earle Barnhart, Hilde Maingay, Nancy Willis, and David Bergmark visited the Island for a few intensely cold and windy days in February 1975, surveying Spry Point on skis to assess the wind and solar energy, exposure and orientation, and views. The bitter winter conditions convinced them of the importance of sheltering buildings from the prevailing winds, and revealed an unexpected potential for solar gain, from sunlight reflected up off surfaces of snow and sea. The crucial need for midwinter energy harvest led Solsearch to reimagine the building as an active mechanism of energy harvest in which "all the surfaces in the structure store heat from the sun."[11] Ark residents, the plants, the fish tanks, and the active solar collectors were "all competing for a place in the sun," so mediating that competition became the overarching design challenge.[12] A key design move was to devote the full southern face of the Ark to the greenhouse, with a wall extending vertically upward from the greenhouse eave supporting a full-length "billboard" of solar collector panels. The unconventional vertical orientation of these collectors was optimized for the combination of low sun angle, reflected sunlight from snow-covered ground, and avoidance of snow accumulation.[13]

North of the greenhouse, an angular wood-clad volume contained the dwelling on a single level above a basement laboratory, workshop, and service space for a Clivus Multrum composter to process organic wastes. The greenhouse floor was also at this basement level, with planting beds to the west and a planting bench along the south wall. Aquaculture was housed in two semi-submerged rectangular concrete tanks to the east, which also served as heat storage for the solar collectors. The greenhouse roof was a sloped glazing system of flat panels, with a complex system of shutters set between the wood joists below. This design was the architects' first response to the parameters and assumptions of the Habitat '76 design. While the food and energy systems were unchanged, the solar collectors were now commercial units and the construction materials and structural systems were more conventional. While much remained to be discovered about how architecture might interact with the biological systems, this first Solsearch design introduced the enduring key concept of building as energy harvester.

Here Solsearch also established the architectural language of the Ark, using a mixed vocabulary of "rough" wood-clad barn- and shed-like structures, contrasted by "smooth"

3.06

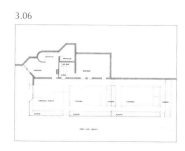

3.07

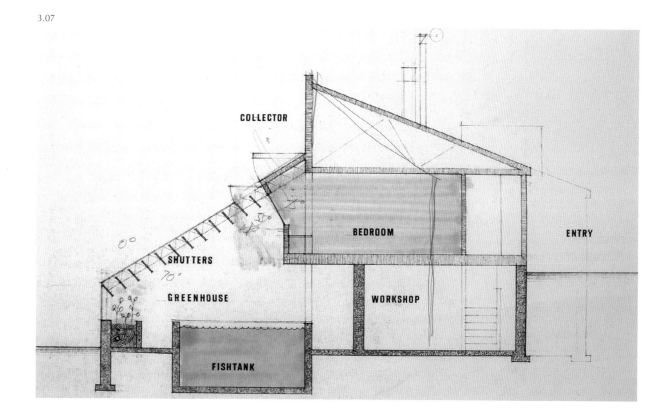

3.08 "The Six-Pack" drawing by Solsearch Architects, *The Journal of the New Alchemists* 4, 1977, 124. This drawing was made after the fact to document the improvised construction of the experimental greenhouse. The basic cross section configuration of translucent south slope and solid north slope with reflective interior surface became a fixture of all future PEI Ark designs.
3.09 David Bergmark with the vertical axis wind turbine beside the Six-Pack, Summer 1975. The turbine provided mechanical power to agitate water in the concrete fish tank.

crystalline expanses of greenhouse and solar panels. The form and detail of the rough wood elements was typical of domestic architecture in the 1970s, exemplified by Condominium No. 1 at Sea Ranch, CA, designed in 1963 by Moore Lyndon Turnbull Whitaker. Charles Moore had been Bergmark's professor at Yale, and his partner Donlyn Lyndon taught Hammarlund at MIT. By the early 1970s, MLTW's aesthetic had become almost a vernacular for architect-designed houses, especially in natural settings. In calling this approach a "modern carpenter gothic" Ole Hammarlund implied that it had become a reflex rather than a conscious choice of style. Solsearch was deliberate in the blunt confrontation of this nostalgic expression with the equally frank image of industrial technology in the greenhouse and solar panels. Rough and smooth, homely and industrial, nostalgic and futuristic – the architectural language of the Ark was a first effort to give visual expression to the similarly dualistic vision of New Alchemy. The message was received by the media and public, who saw the building as a "Space-Age Ark" and a "Habitat Concept for the Future."[14]

The Six-Pack: Testing the Greenhouse, May 1975

> The New Alchemy-Solsearch association has become symbiotic as the architects started delving into biology, energy conservation and appropriate technologies while we in turn learned about architectural problems and possibilities. Since bioshelters are not just structures this relationship was critical in creating a working Ark.[15]

John Todd's assessment indicates the intensity and scope of the architectural-biological design collaboration. In addition to the first sketch designs for the PEI Ark, New Alchemy and Solsearch explored the interaction of architectural form with food and energy systems in a small test building on the Cape Cod farm. Over the course of a week, Bergmark and Hammarlund improvised a greenhouse shelter over an existing concrete fish tank, with minimal design sketches and details resolved on the fly.[16] The result was an asymmetrical arrangement of a sloped south wall that used translucent fiberglass "Kalwall" sheets, site-formed into a series of barrel vaults evoking beer cans. Earle Barnhart first called it the "Six-Pack."[17] An insulated north roof reduced heat loss, and its interior surface was painted white to reflect low winter sun down onto the plants and fish tank.[18] Apart from the Kalwall vaults, the construction was conventional, with stick-frame carpentry on concrete foundations. The space was partly recessed into the ground for insulation and geothermal gains. The east and west end-walls of the southern half of the volume were clad in flat Kalwall, laid against diagonal studs spanning from a centreline column to the rake of the roof, intended to evoke a vision of tree limbs;

two symmetrical Kalwall panels lit the upper part of the shingled half of the ends.[19] The southern parts of the end walls were glazed with high-level shutters for ventilation which sported the Solsearch yin-yang sun logo. Aquaculture in the concrete fish tank occupied half the Six-Pack floor area, with the rest given to deep soil planting beds. Plant containers hung from the walls. Terraced exterior planters provided earth shelter on the northern exposure and supported a vertical axis wind turbine for water pumping and aeration.

The Six-Pack greenhouse served as a robust proving ground for the integration of architecture and biology, yielding important data about crop and fish yields through the seasons. Experiments in natural pest management and nutrient flows between agriculture and aquaculture gave the team confidence to scale up the project. The hands-on design-build process provided the New Alchemy/Solsearch design team vivid and immediate feedback about real-world implications of design and material choices. Six-Pack's configuration of maximum exposure to the south and maximum enclosure to the north with internal solar reflection proved effective for the New Alchemy food systems, and would form the basis for the design of the subsequent Arks. Air temperatures at the greenhouse ridge exceeded 100° F, showing the potential for hot air harvest as a heat source. But heat storage in the fish tank was poor, and significant windmill energy was needed to counter thermal stratification in the water.[20] Further, the Kalwall vaults were deemed too fragile for the harsh winds and snow of Prince Edward Island.[21]

During the build, extra Kalwall sheets were improvised into two vertical cylinders to create an aquaculture environment. These tanks, dubbed "Suntube" solar ponds, were an opportunistic experiment, and their shape and large surface area proved highly effective at promoting algae growth.[22] This instance of symbiotic bio-architectural development not only enabled better self-managed tank environments, but also integrated the fish tanks into the solar heating system. Six-Pack trials showed these cylindrical ponds to be highly effective passive solar storage devices, with the dark algae blooms significantly enhancing the heat absorption and transfer capacity – hence John Todd's term "low-temperature solar furnaces."[23] Engaging the food systems more generally in providing building energy services could only have come from this sort of deep collaboration. The Six-Pack's most important yield was an architectural and spatial vocabulary capable of serving the biological systems while providing a satisfying human environment. Here, New Alchemy and Solsearch discovered the spatial and spiritual qualities of the greenhouse space, which inspire the design of the interconnected kitchen/kitchen greenhouse space as the living heart of the PEI Ark.

3.10 "Suntube" solar fish pond demonstration at New Alchemy, Cape Cod, MA, 1977.
3.11 The Six-Pack with a "Suntube" solar fish pond in the foreground, Summer 1975. "Suntube" ponds were improvised using extra Kalwall sheets from the greenhouse enclosure.

3.12

3.13

The solar greenhouse need not function solely as a means of food production….
It is a psychological boon to those who actively become part of its ecosystem…
a joy to step, trowel in hand, into a balmy greenhouse smelling of earth and herbs
and marigolds, even in the coldest months of the winter.[24]

The "Bioshelter" Concept and Suntek Film

During the Six-Pack trials, John Todd came across an *Architecture Plus* article on a concept for an integrated biological-spatial system by MIT scientists Day Chahroudi and Sean Wellesley-Miller.[25] Like the Ark concept, the "bioshelter" was inspired by biological systems, capable of producing its own energy and climate, treating its own wastes and growing food for the residents, and would include human habitation; the enclosure would actively participate in environmental control.[26] But where Solsearch adapted recognizable building elements and materials to create an architecture of energy harvest, Chahroudi and Wellesley-Miller staked their hopes for an active enclosure on a single "miracle" material, their own patented Suntek membrane. This multi-layer polymer film would provide thermal insulation and selective transmission of solar radiation, enabling a stable interior temperature while admitting light energy.[27] Their drawings showed large-span, minimally structured, free-form enclosures, wrapped in a clear membrane – more like covered landscapes than buildings. Such bioshelters would transcend individual buildings-as-shelters to provide "large span structures … to free man and his architecture from climate."[28] A scaleless diagram of the basic bioshelter idea recalls Buckminster Fuller's proposal for a dome over midtown Manhattan. Todd gave Earle Barnhart a reprint of the article, marked: "Earle, I got this for you – fantastic."

Though committed to a building solution rather than a free-form enclosure, New Alchemy and Solsearch were interested in the Suntek membrane as a form of "transparent insulation" that might solve the heat loss challenges of greenhouses. For testing in the Six-Pack, several layers of Suntek film were assembled in a roll sized to match the joist spacing, joined along the edges with a reinforced tape connector-spacer that enabled the membrane to be stapled to the structure. Though the inventors sought a robust membrane with a thirty-year life, in reality Suntek was fragile and depended on the Kalwall vaults for protection from the elements. Ole Hammarlund reported that the film was very fussy to work with, and so fragile that growing cucumber plants could puncture the inner layer.[29] Suntek film was shown and noted as "transparent insulation" on the Ark design drawings up to August 1975, but ultimately rejected after the problematic trial in the Six-Pack. Though they dropped the film, the New Alchemists retained "bioshelter" as a generic name for their integrative structures, using it as a companion term to "Ark" for years to come.

3.12 Bioshelter visualization, from "Bioshelter," *Architecture Plus* (November-December 1974): 90. The article envisioned vast free-form environments conditioned by Suntek membranes. The membrane proved fragile in the Six-Pack trials and was abandoned, though the New Alchemists adopted "bioshelter" as a description for their Arks.
3.13 View of the Six-Pack at New Alchemy's Cape Cod farm, Summer 1975. The geodesic dome was an earlier approach to enclosing the aquaculture environment; beyond the dome is the Sailwing windmill.

Second Solsearch Ark Design:
Three Sheds and a Greenhouse, June 1975

Learning from the Six-Pack trials and the Spry Point site visit, the next Ark design focused even more on the energy harvest and architectural potential of the greenhouse. The building form was radically simplified in response to the challenge of constructing a large and complex Ark bioshelter on a remote site with hostile winters. Construction needed to be within the repertoire of Island builders; furthermore, Solsearch felt that the forms and materials ought to be "familiar" to the Spry Point community, to minimize the sense of the Ark as an alien intrusion. Hammarlund described the architectural language as "modern carpenter gothic" composed in assemblies of simple volumes with single-sloped roofs, clad in shingle or clapboard stained dark brown, and trimmed with flat eave and corner boards and window surrounds.[30] Rather than a public-friendly perspective drawing, this design was presented using an axonometric projection, a more abstract architectural convention, along with a simple cardboard model, which suggests that the design was for internal study and may not have been presented outside the design team.

3.15

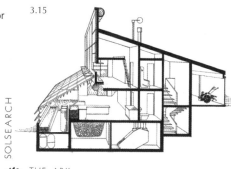

3.14

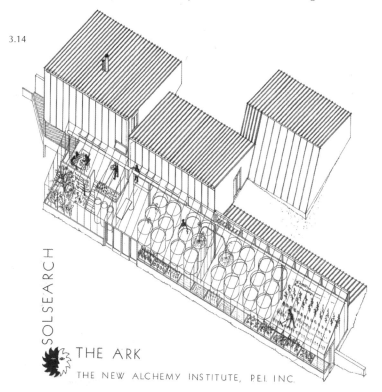

3.14 "Solsearch – The Ark," axonometric view of the "Three Sheds" design, scale 1 inch = 8 feet. Drawing by Ole Hammarlund, Solsearch Architects, ink on mylar, ca. June 1975. A composition of three shed-like closed volumes sits to the north of an extensive east-west greenhouse. The design introduces the interconnected arrangement of dining space, kitchen and kitchen greenhouse that was a compelling feature of the final Ark. Aquaculture is entirely conducted in "Suntube" solar ponds.

3.15 "Solsearch – The Ark," section perspective view of the "Three Sheds" design. Solsearch Architects, ink on mylar, ca. June 1975. This drawing explores the interconnected kitchen greenhouse and kitchen/dining area of the dwelling.

The greenhouse occupied the entire southern exposure, again with a billboard of vertical solar collectors above. Within the greenhouse, the inside north wall adopted the Six-Pack's white-painted slope to reflect low winter sun onto the plants and fish. Planting areas were at the east end, and aquaculture occupied the central zone of the greenhouse; this arrangement in full depth north-south zones provided less optimal sunlight conditions than the eventual east-west organization of the final design. An array of cylindrical "Suntube" solar ponds, as developed for the Six-Pack, took the place of concrete fish ponds. These tanks and the planting beds served as passive solar heat storage, while a rock vault stored heat harvested by a duct from the top of the greenhouse. The greenhouse was enclosed with a commercial glazing system; Solsearch felt certain that the custom-fabricated Kalwall barrel vaults of the Six-Pack would not withstand the Island's winter conditions.[31]

Behind the greenhouse were three shed-form volumes, containing the dwelling, laboratory, and barn. Each shed was nestled into the slope with its south face given over to solar collectors. The barn shed was pulled back from the north side of the greenhouse to create a sheltered service court open to the east; this also substantially increased the surface area and resulting winter heat losses. The south walls of the dwelling unit and laboratory sheds extended up past the eave of the greenhouse, accommodating a vertical "billboard" of solar collector panels. Prominent exterior ducts fed hot air from these collectors down into a second rock storage vault under the dwelling, serving the human-inhabited spaces. At the west end, the dwelling unit peeked slightly beyond the greenhouse, giving the human inhabitants a bit of southern exposure. Its lower corner was carved away to create a sheltered outdoor terrace, which extended inside through patio doors, and projected slightly into the greenhouse to create an interconnected volume of kitchen, dining area and kitchen greenhouse. This space was very close to the final built design, right down to details such as the in-counter herb planter and the steps down to the fish tanks and planting area. Here the satisfying enjoyment of the greenhouse space by the human inhabitants, a "discovery" of the Six-Pack, became a thematic element of the architecture. Hammarlund reflected "we all became more and more enchanted with the idea that the greenhouse space was an important space for living, not just for production."[32]

Third Solsearch Ark Design: Reintegration, July-August 1975
The organization and basic architectural vocabulary of the "Three Sheds" scheme were carried into the next design iteration. To reduce the exterior surface area and consequent heat losses, the sheds were reassembled into a single volume, with the greenhouse

retaining its southern position. The vertical solar collector billboard was divided into three functional sections, each with panels using either air or water as the heat transfer medium. A stepped up section of billboard at the west end marked the extent of the dwelling unit below; prominent exterior ducts transferred the hot air to a rock vault below for dwelling heat. Immediately to the east, a band of laterally oriented panels heated domestic water; then a section of air transfer panels provided space heat for the greenhouse. The eastern third of the collector billboard used water transfer panels to heat the aquaculture tanks.

The greenhouse was re-organized to place the Suntube aquaculture tanks along the north side, shaded from the high summer sun, with planting beds down the centre and a planting bench along the south wall where solar exposure was maximized. The planting bench sat above the duct distributing hot air from the rock vault. The greenhouse structure was conventional lumber framing using 2x12 joists, with two distinct enclosure systems. Above the kitchen greenhouse was "double glazing" of insulating glass units above pivoting insulated aluminum shutters fitted between the wood joists. The commercial greenhouse showed "acrylic double glazing" over "transparent insulation" (the Suntek membrane, not yet discredited by the Six-Pack trials). This acrylic double glazing formed part of a manufactured greenhouse enclosure system comprising the four-foot-wide extruded cellular acrylic panels with integral insulating air chambers, set in a grid of aluminum mullions, gaskets and seals.[33] Greenhouse ventilation used custom-fabricated panels set between the joists at the top of the slope, with conventional awning windows at the low southern wall.

Overall, the trajectory of design development was towards an ever-simpler form, containing a smaller volume with a reduced surface area to volume ratio, and with these surfaces increasingly optimized for energy harvest. The variety of materials and systems were incrementally reduced, and conventional, commercially available materials supplanted custom and unconventional ones wherever possible, making the realization of the Ark's "revolutionary building format" feasible and economical in the rural context of eastern Prince Edward Island.[34] Solsearch produced a full set of detailed design development drawings of this version, dated August 1975. They showed a building structure and enclosure using conventional light stick framing with clapboard siding and metal roofing, with careful attention to continuity of insulation. Details were provided where the arrangements were complex, such as the framing of the upper walls of the greenhouse above the long beam and the line of support posts. The airtight envelope design was shown in careful details of the main junctions. Schematic diagrams of the wood framing layouts at walls and floors showed the architects'

3.16 Ark for PEI, design sketch of the third Solsearch Ark design showing the kitchen and family greenhouse. Drawing by Ole Hammarlund, Solsearch Architects, ink and marker on mylar, Summer 1975.

Ark for PEI design development drawings, Solsearch Architects, pencil on tracing paper, 6 August 1975. These drawings show the Ark as developed in the "systems model," and were used as the basis for construction. The energy systems changes led to numerous changes in detail and systems that were resolved on site as the work progressed.

3.17

3.18

3.19

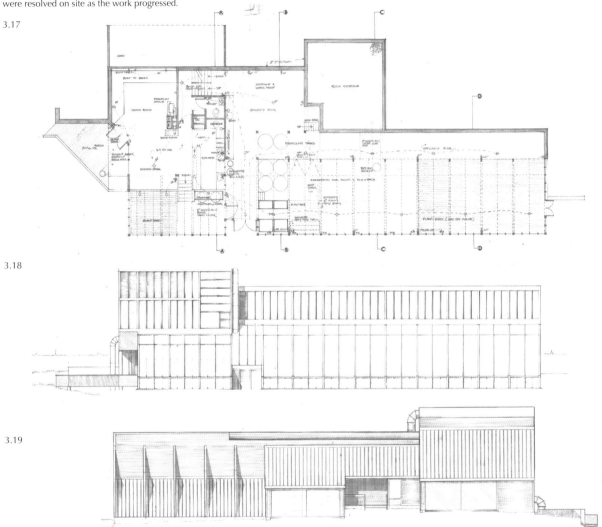

3.17 "Main Floor Plan," scale 1 inch = 4 feet. Suntube solar fish ponds occupy the full depth of the central part of the commercial greenhouse, with the deep planting beds at the east. In the final Ark this became two rows of ponds across the full width of the greenhouse north of the columns (which are shifted four feet south), and deep planting beds across the full width south of the columns.

3.18 "South Elevation," scale 1 inch = 4 feet. Prominent ducts serve the air heat transfer medium; the billboard of collectors above the commercial greenhouse is set back slightly from those of the dwelling (eliminated in the final building). The solar collectors heating domestic water are distinguished as horizontal rectangles.

3.19 "North Elevation," scale 1 inch = 4 feet. The north elevation is topped by a tall parapet with horizontal air ducts serving the solar collector panels (eliminated in the final Ark). Complicated buttresses support the wall behind the east part of the greenhouse; these were simplified to a single sloped roof surface during construction.

attention to the information needs of the Island builders.

Visually, the final Ark design was a mix of the familiar – wood siding and sloped roofs – and the futuristic – translucent greenhouse and solar panels. Both New Alchemy and Solsearch were sensitive to the symbolic and expressive challenge of such a new approach to ecological building. Thinking about the people who would occupy or visit the building, the architects observed that "no effort has been made to conceal the energy systems within the envelope of the building; the idea was rather to express the systems visually in an attempt to develop a new aesthetic and consciousness for energy producing and conserving structures."[35] John Todd echoed this thought and noted the challenge of relating the Ark to its context:

> All along there has been considerable discussion of the ark's aesthetics. It is to be situated in an extraordinarily beautiful place on the edge of the sea and must be worthy of the site. The architects were especially sensitive to our request that it prove a powerful statement for an emerging solar aesthetic, for the Ark must not only work, but echo the slogan of the Province – "The Place to Be."[36]

The Quest for Energy Systems Expertise

In contrast to the symbiotic collaboration between New Alchemy and Solsearch, the team's relations with their government sponsors were fraught. Midway through the development of this third Solsearch Ark design, the team had committed six months of intense effort to the development of the Ark but remained without a formal funding agreement.[37] This gamble seemed to turn to disaster in early summer 1975, when on July 4 the federal government suddenly cancelled the Canadian Urban Demonstration Program.[38] Within days, a telegram from Minister Barney Danson assured them that funds would be provided to the Ark project from other federal sources. Environment Canada's Advanced Concepts Centre was named the project manager and "scientific authority" for the Ark on behalf of the Canadian government. Advanced Concepts' support was motivated primarily by the promise of spin-off knowledge, which they hoped could mobilize the rapid development of a Canadian solar energy industry with export potential. To conceive, design, build, and operate the Ark would achieve the stated goal of a self-sufficient bioshelter; along the way the process would generate substantial research results on alternative energy systems. Advanced Concepts hired Scanada Engineering in Ottawa for engineering and technical reviews of the Ark, in addition to the Technical Review panel. Solsearch built a cardboard study model showing the Ark's form and systems, which accompanied the detailed construction and systems drawings, presented at a major review in late summer 1975. David Bergmark described the review process:

3.20

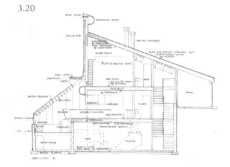

3.21

3.20 "Sections – Preliminary," scale 1 inch = 4 feet. Complex aluminum shutters below the south sloped roof of the greenhouse were eliminated in the final Ark, as were the custom upper vent panels set flush with the roof.

3.21 Ark for PEI, "systems model" of the third Solsearch Ark design, scale 1 inch = 4 feet. Model by Solsearch Architects, cardboard, basswood, plastic and paper, ca. August 1975. This model was used in meetings with government officials, the technical review panel, and the engineering review consultants. The main "billboard" of solar panels uses air as the heat transfer medium. Large white ducts flanking the residence zone connect the panels to the rock storage vault below ground.

We used this [model] when we met with the engineers to go over the concepts to project what successes we would have in terms of a northern climate building. We were able to demonstrate our ideas, many of which [engineers] had not relied on for many years. They'd relied on mechanical equipment to provide energy in buildings, rather than relying on nature to provide that energy.[39]

This third Solsearch Ark design was the first version seen by the Technical Review panel since Barnhart and Maingay's original design, and answered many of the concerns identified back in January, clearing the way for the project to move ahead.[40] But while meetings with the consultant engineers and Technical Review panel led to project approvals, they also showed that the New Alchemists were asking questions beyond the ken of these experts, who were learning about these untried or long-unused approaches to building energy along with Solsearch and New Alchemy. For the most part, the design team were left to their own research; they worked from first principles in validating the systems. All those involved recall a grinding anxiety about whether the systems would work, and whether enough energy could be harvested to cope with the Island winter.[41]

Following the technical review, Solsearch continued to refine their energy analysis of the Ark design. In early fall they came to the realization that the air-based solar heating system was not up to the task.[42] The plan to send heated air in ducts from the "billboard" of solar collectors to the rock storage vault entailed multiple heat exchanges – from sun to collector to air ducts to rocks for storage, then from rocks to air ducts to dwelling room for distribution – and each exchange was a point of heat loss. Collectors directly heating water for storage in an insulated tank would be much more efficient in terms of exchange losses, and more importantly, water in tanks has five times the specific heat capacity of air and rock vault storage.[43] To assist with the change from air to water collectors, the architects turned to Everett M. Barber, one of Bergmark's building systems professors at Yale. Barber provided information on systems configurations, temperature-actuated valves, and data for use in calculations based on his practical industry experience as the manufacturer of Sunworks solar collectors. Sunworks would eventually supply the panels for the main collector "billboard" of the PEI Ark.[44] Even with the change to a more efficient transfer and storage medium, calculations showed that the full "billboard" of panels would be needed to heat the dwelling. Fortunately the Six-Pack trials showed that direct solar gains were enough to heat the aquaculture tanks, and that there would be sufficient heat available from passive solar gains at the peak of the greenhouse roof to serve the greenhouse rock storage vault. This allowed all the vertical collectors to be devoted to the dwelling unit; insulated water tanks for heat storage would take the place of the rock vault beneath the dwelling.

3.22 Ole Hammarlund and David Bergmark studying the Ark systems model, summer 1975.
3.23 Ark for PEI, "systems model" of the third Solsearch Ark design, scale 1 inch = 4 feet. Replica model constructed by David Bergmark and Ole Hammarlund, cardboard, basswood, plastic and paper, 2015-16.

This change had ripple effects through the entire building design, from foundation configuration upwards, but with site preparations under way there was no time for Solsearch to prepare a comprehensive set of drawings for a revised design.[45] Since the overall massing, architectural details, greenhouse layout, and site planning would be mostly unchanged, the August 1975 drawings were used as the basis for starting construction. A continual stream of changes to arrangements, details, and systems were resolved on site as the work progressed. The foundations were revised to provide the water tanks for heat storage below the dwelling. The greenhouse roof was simplified by specifying "Rohaglas" brand acrylic double glazing with an insulating value of R1.8, comparable to sealed insulating glass units. This eliminated the need for the problematic Suntek insulating film over the commercial greenhouse.[46] The Rohaglas system also replaced the insulating glass over the kitchen greenhouse, where the insulated aluminum shutters were also dropped, to avoid any reduction of light penetration.[47] The custom upper vent panels were replaced by conventional greenhouse vent windows mounted vertically in the wall above. Solar panels for domestic hot water heating changed from a vertical array to a sloped array, for better year-round solar harvest. Overall, details and materials were simplified and refined. Managing this on-the-fly process was not entirely alien to the architects, given their backgrounds in design-build and renovation work, and following on the recent improvised construction processes of the Six-Pack, but it would add substantial pressure to Solsearch's construction coordination role. On the positive side, the extent of the design changes from the systems revisions (and further material substitutions and refinements) would have been a nightmare of paperwork and contract changes if a conventional general contractor had been involved.

Construction in the Community, September 1975 – September 1976

Solsearch's efforts to make the Ark construction feasible for Island builders seemed successful at first. With help from Andy Wells, an agreement in principle was reached with Schurmans, an established Island contractor.[48] But the delays in federal funding and approvals pushed the start date back, forcing winter construction and bumping the final price to more than double the budget. In order to complete the Ark in time to present it at Habitat '76, the New Alchemy Institute took over the project management role in September 1975. Solsearch became both architect and general contractor, leading Island tradespeople and builders on site.[49] The carpentry and construction backgrounds of Bergmark and Hammarlund now became crucial in steering the building process through unexpected challenges and ingenious solutions, and resolving any remaining design issues.

3.24 Builders from the eastern Prince Edward Island community, Winter 1976, including George Christianson (far left), Lemmie Chaisson (far right).

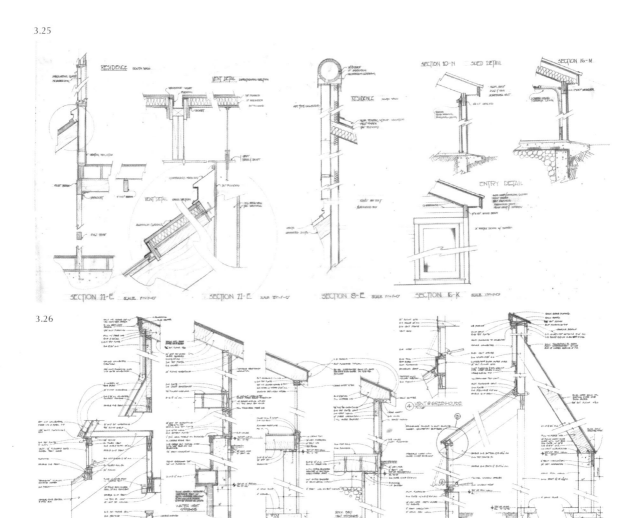

3.25 "Wall Sections," Ark for PEI design development drawing, scale 1 inch = 1 foot. Solsearch Architects, pencil on tracing paper, 6 August 1975. This drawing shows details of the summer 1975 Ark design which used air as the solar heat exchange medium, and was used as the basis for construction.

3.26 "Wall Sections," Ark for PEI construction drawing, scale 1 inch = 1 foot. Solsearch Architects, Pencil on Mylar, dated October 1975 (actual date Fall 1976). This drawing documents the final resolution of the details as built. Though dated October 1975, this was in fact drawn in fall 1976 after construction was complete. In general, the details as built were simpler and used more conventional materials and methods than those shown on the August drawings.

In October 1975, David Bergmark and Nancy Willis moved to the Island to oversee construction, renting a house across the cove from the Spry Point site. Bergmark led the construction work through the first winter, while Ole Hammarlund stayed at the New Alchemy farm to build the Cape Cod Ark. Hammarlund travelled regularly to Spry Point, including overseeing the crucial moment when the long beam and upper wall of the greenhouse were erected above the support posts. The builders came mostly from eastern PEI, notably Jim and Steve Cheverie from Souris.[50] Relations between locals and the newcomers were convivial but assumptions sometimes diverged. One local man offered to collect the rock for the heat storage vault, returning with a car trunk full of odd stones; when told this was vastly inadequate, he informed Solsearch that there wasn't that much rock on the whole island.[51] Local ingenuity showed up in the dry well installation, with a backhoe interring an old junked car. An Island fibreglass boat builder was found to locally manufacture the "Suntube" solar ponds.[52] As the building shaped up, Willis led the installation of the greenhouse food system elements, and all the while took the lead in establishing good relations with the Spry Point community. Her mix of "bingo diplomacy" and "bikini diplomacy" earned her the nickname "The Ark Angel" among the neighbours. She reflected:

> We came in here like a bomb, weirdoes in shorts and boots, but there was an acceptance. We landed in this little rural community, and they were so good to us. These people just embraced us, we played cards, we went to the community centre, we all really fit into the community, even though we were totally weird from their perspective. And it worked. It became a little bit of a New Alchemy North, in the sense that the people that were building it took ownership of the Ark, and they still talk about it.[53]

Everyone shared the urgency of finishing the Ark on time. Extended work hours, occasional work on Sundays, and efforts beyond the letter of the contract were common. Willis recalled the just-installed metal roof coming away in a fierce windstorm late one evening in December 1975. The rescue was managed more quickly because several of the builders were eating a late supper at the Bergmark/Willis house directly across the cove from the Ark, so everyone was able to head to the site together.

The Carnival of Completion, Summer 1976

Even with the combined efforts, passion, and goodwill of the New Alchemists and their Spry Point and Island collaborators, the construction of the Ark proceeded slowly. A newspaper progress report in late winter 1976 speaks favourably about the effectiveness of the passive solar heating of the greenhouse, despite the fact that the enclosure was

3.27 Local contractors installing a junked car to serve as the dry well for greywater disposal from the sinks and laundry, Fall 1975. This was a typical eastern Island approach to creating a septic tank.

still temporary polyethylene sheets rather than the final greenhouse glazing.[54] Winter construction meant that some tasks could not be done in sequence, and others only with expensive temporary heat. It also meant unplanned increases in costs. Some efforts to reduce costs led to delays: for example, the slow but ultimately successful diversion of surplus cedar siding from a larger order for Island liquor stores. On the other hand, a boxcar of fibreglass insulation donated by Manville enabled the roof insulation levels to be doubled.[55] Hammarlund moved to PEI in April 1976, and was joined in June by his wife Fausta and four children. The pace picked up as many New Alchemists began commuting regularly to the Island to assist.

Word of the Ark made its way out through Appropriate Technology and counterculture channels, and over the summer of 1976 the population of the Ark site on Spry Point grew steadily, reaching a peak in early September. Nancy Willis recalled:

> About a month before the end, people started arriving from all across the continent, and some from Europe as well. We had to set up a tent area, but they didn't depend on us, they were all on their own. They would come in and volunteer, and it was hectic for David and Ole because they had to try to find stuff that they could do. But we were really thrilled with it because it meant that what we were thinking and doing was paying off.[56]

Any visitor with useful skills who offered to help was set to work. Over the last weeks, with hundreds of people on the site, the Ark was brought to completion in a festival atmosphere. Nancy Jack Todd saw the scene as consistent with the New Alchemy spirit:

> As it has always been with New Alchemy gatherings, the people who arrived, for whatever reasons, were varied and wonderful. Many of the long-haired young appeared in vans, on foot or with packsacks. … Academics wielded hammers and paint brushes beside poets and homesteaders. Island neighbours gave up Sundays to stay on the job.[57]

Among the incomers was J. Baldwin, a leading figure in the Appropriate Technology world, *Whole Earth Catalog* contributor, and co-editor with Stewart Brand of its successor *Co-evolution Quarterly*. He and his partner Kathleen Whitacre arrived ten days before the opening; they installed the greenhouse vent window operators after the instructions went missing. Baldwin recalls a "swirling uproar of people all working like mad … there is a lot of local curiosity, and consequently a steady stream of visitors … I am amazed at the high level of questions asked, and also by the hope and excitement showing in the eyes of many visitors."[58] Premier Alex Campbell paid an anxious visit to the site in the final week. Andy Wells convinced a provincial highway contractor working nearby to divert heavy equipment to the site for a day, sculpting the wind

3.28 Framing the Ark for PEI, Fall 1975. The Ark used conventional light lumber stick framing, though the architects provided detailed layout drawings of every column, stud, and joist.
3.29 The camping area on the Ark site for volunteer workers and visitors, September 1976, with Chris Willis and an unidentified adult (front); Sven, Jurgen and Ate Atema (children in middle); and Earle Barnhart (at the tent door).

deflecting berm and pond north of the Ark and hydroseeding the ground.[59] Everyone worked through the night before the opening. Building tasks were completed, such as finishing the floors and painting the woodwork. The greenhouse beds were planted and the fish tanks set up and populated. A crane was diverted from a church steeple job to install the Hydrowind turbine. With a last desperate push, locals on tractors buried the final piles of construction debris, the grounds were tidied, and paths were laid out from the helicopter landing to the Ark porch. Baldwin described the last moments:

> Locals appear with a huge tent and literally thousands of sandwiches made by neighbours so the reception will "speak well of the people from Little Pond." … The Ark looks like something from another planet. Spotless! Flowers everywhere inside. Fresh fruit. John and his crew have planted trees all over the place! Some crew has laid out hundreds of feet of neat gravel paths in the mud. The Clivus Multrum toilets smell as sweet as clover. The indoor farm-gardens are alive with little sprouts. There are Tilapia swimming around in one of the tanks. The whole place glitters in the morning sun. A beautiful day in the midst of a rainy season. A fresh wind comes up and the Hydrowind whizzes, actually making power for the first time. The Prime Minister alights from his Huey.[60]

3.29

The Ark's Life and Legacy

4

In the wake of the opening day circus and the all-night party, at the end of months of intense work surrounded by hundreds of volunteers and curiosity seekers, the Ark people may have hoped to be left in peace to carry on with the careful work of operating and monitoring the Ark as an integrated living system. Instead, the carnival atmosphere would intensify, with unceasing interest from around the world. Frictions between satisfying a curious public and fulfilling the research agenda would prove challenging. At the same time, shifts in the political climate would see official culture push the countercultural innovators to the margins of their own project.

The morning after the opening party was the autumn equinox. The New Alchemists gathered for ceremonies that were more private and spiritual, one led by Keptin John Joe Sark that welcomed the project to the Mi'kmaw district of Epekwitk;[1] the other by David Spangler of the Lorian Association, a spiritual group dedicated to advancing the wholeness of humanity with the earth. For Nancy Jack Todd, these moments were an articulation of "what we hoped the Ark and ideas like it might come to mean – of a dream of a renewed understanding of the larger patterns of life and of the human place within such patterns."[2] As John and Nancy Jack Todd and most other New Alchemists headed back to Cape Cod, David Bergmark, Nancy Willis, and Nancy's children Chris and Meredith were left to conduct the Ark's "living experiment." Willis was the Ark Manager, overseeing the operation of the building and tending the food systems; she was also Assistant Director of "The New Alchemy Institute – Prince Edward Island." New Alchemy employees at the PEI Ark included Linda Gilkeson, working on biological pest controls in the greenhouse; Wayne Vantoever on aquaculture; and Joe Seale on the Hydrowind.[3]

Media interest in that first year was rabid, and the Ark life became a life lived in public. An unexpected task for the Ark family was managing the relentless stream of visitors – from sceptical hippie-gawkers and alternative technology enthusiasts to the

4.02

4.01 The play structure to the west of the Ark, Fall 1976. From left, Shira Hammarlund climbing the pole; Nooni Hammarlund in the low swing; Carla MacDonald in the high swing.
4.02 Distant view towards the Ark from the northwest, showing the earth mound sheltering the closed north face of the building from winter winds, ca. 1977.

4.03

4.04

tourists who made Spry Point a stop on the family vacation. The Ark was a futuristic contrast to the homely traditions of the Island's other famous house: that of Anne of Green Gables from Lucy Maud Montgomery's eponymous novel. While clearly not the kind of place where Anne Shirley would have lived, the Ark's pursuit of self-sufficiency was in keeping with the aims of the Cuthbert farm. The Ark's melding of advanced technology with traditional ideals of place, sufficiency, and meaningful work resonated with many visitors, providing a vivid experience of an alternative to a globalizing consumerist world.

The Social Vision of the Ark

Echoing Marshall McLuhan's observations about the counterculture's "re-tribalization of society," historian Ian MacKay argues that the social alienation of 20th century industrial modernity created a reactionary response in the form of liberal anti-modernism, which he describes as an "individualistic thirst for an existence released from the iron cage of modernity, a world re-enchanted by history, by nature, by the mysterious."[4] The Ark satisfied this desire among its visitors, while showing that a re-enchanted world need not entail a reactionary return to a socially problematic past. Instead, the Ark offered a vision of the interconnectedness of natural processes, its inhabitants and, in its final vision, local communities. John Todd believed the Ark was primarily a teaching tool for the liberation of humanity:

> Living in the Ark can be an extraordinary experience. Living and working in a structure where the sun, the wind, architecture and ecosystems are operating in concert has affected most of us. It seems to foretell what the future could bring. Each of us involved in the project would like to live one day in an Ark-inspired bioshelter. Its psychological impact is not easily articulated. The Ark, as a humanly-derived ecosystem, creates a sense of wholeness and integrity engendered by a high degree of self sufficiency.[5]

Nancy Jack Todd argued that Ark life was a feminist life. She noted that the Ark design process, by directly involving New Alchemy's women, challenged the dominant male-mindedness (and male-blindedness) of modern technological thinking. Todd observed

> a feminine tendency … toward more compactness and economy of design with space for children's activities that is not isolated from work areas. This could encourage more direct participation by everyone in household activities …. Overall, the women's reaction to the possibilities inherent in the bioshelter was of relief at contemplating greater independence from the technological determinism we still experience.[6]

4.03 A tour group at the Ark, 1977. A cross-section of Canadian society and guests from around the world visited the Ark over the first few years.
4.04 The farmhouse-style dining table at the heart of the Ark, open to the kitchen greenhouse beyond.
From A Most Prudent Ark, 1977, 12.

Constance Mungall, writing to Canadian women in *Chatelaine*, shared Nancy Jack Todd's sense of the meaning and value of the Ark lifestyle. Her article envisions family life within the Ark as engaged with place and community, a powerful antidote to creeping suburban *ennui* in the mid-1970s. "Could an ordinary person run the Ark? … With the 1,900 square foot greenhouse and the 30 fish tanks producing cash crops, it would be a full-time job – but one many women would enjoy – at home with kids, but producing and earning."[7] By the 1980s, consumerism would co-opt feminism in a very different solution to the isolation of the suburban housewife – holding down a second job in a two-income family, with an accompanying explosion of consumerism. From a present-day perspective, the Ark life seems a more fully liberating route for both families and the planet, especially since the living experiment featured Bergmark and Willis sharing the for-income work and the child-rearing responsibilities in the Ark.

Not all responses to the Ark were positive, and some criticism came from unexpected quarters. Managing visitors quickly became a major distraction from the research and monitoring work that, for the New Alchemists, was the real point of the Ark – though they were themselves responsible for this research/demonstration conflict. Their original proposal to the Urban Demonstration Program emphasized the public demonstration and education potentials of the Ark. Furthermore, in August 1975, John Todd drew up a proposal to the Island government to expand the offerings on site to include new and retrofitted houses, multiple forms of wind turbine, and expanded agri/aquaculture and tree planting demonstrations that promised to create a tourist-oriented ecological architecture interpretation centre.[8] To handle the conflict, they implemented the Cape Cod practice of opening the site only one day per week (Sundays) for public tours. The local community remained welcome to visit at all times. Frustrated visitors resented the restricted hours, especially those who came to see the Ark out of a sense of affinity with its mission and goals, which hurt the Ark's reputation among its natural supporters. Some of these enthusiasts were also disenchanted by the full bourgeois complement of modern appliances. But the New Alchemists argued that these conveniences showed the general public that an ecological lifestyle need not require primitive conditions or hardship.[9]

Documenting the Ark Experiment
Despite the distractions of visitors and media attention, New Alchemy and Solsearch continued to carry out their research and monitoring program. They obtained important performance data for building energy systems that were widely touted as alternatives to the status quo, but for which few had experience of actual performance. In the best

4.05 Nancy Willis working at the planting bench in the commercial greenhouse, Winter 1977. Interpretive signage (such as on the post between windows) was added to support self-directed tours.
4.06 Gates at the entry to the site with the Ark in the distance, ca. 1976. Restricted visiting hours frustrated some visitors, especially those from far away. Neighbours were welcome at all times.

4.07

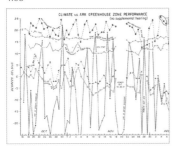

4.08

4.07 View to the dining room, with the kitchen and family greenhouse beyond, 1977.
4.08 Logging interior temperatures against exterior temperatures at the Ark, from the Ark Report of December 1976 (69). The effectiveness of the Ark energy systems in maintaining the interior climate despite challenging weather is shown where the outside temperature flatlines at the bottom of the graph (-25 degrees celsius or lower) on November 19 and 20, the famous "winter storm." Lack of power meant no interior data was recorded, but the data points before and after show minimal loss of heat during the storm.

tradition of the New Alchemists, the lessons drawn from experience and experiment were shared with those who wished to put them into practice, in their *Journal* and in official reports.[10] An extensive *Final Report* went to the Canadian government at the end of December 1976, barely three months into operation, documenting in detail the origin, philosophy, and design process of the project. Extensive technical drawings, made in the fall of 1976 after the opening, document the architecture and systems as-built, reflecting the many on-the-fly changes made through construction and commissioning.[11] Data logged by 32 sensors installed in the Ark were used to correlate outside weather against interior environment conditions, temperatures in the water and rock heat storage, and the productivity of the greenhouse systems.

Impressively, the interwoven architecture and biology enabled the Ark to exceed expectations for heating autonomy. Starting in late September 1976, the solar systems were unable to fully charge the water and rock storage with heat before the arrival of the winter, yet the Ark was able to weather a three-day November storm and black-out with temperatures below -5° C and winds over 50 kilometres per hour. Heat from the "Suntube" aquaculture tanks stabilized the greenhouse temperatures well above freezing; the living unit drew warmth from the family garden, supplemented by the wood stove burning late afternoon until midnight.[12] The storm also showed that considerable heat was transmitted to the main level of the living unit directly from the storage tanks, and warm air rose from the family garden greenhouse on sunny days, resulting in little need for the ducted heating system.[13]

A highlight of the report is a comparison between the Ark and a conventional modern house, which the New Alchemists characterized as a leaky building that consumed disproportionate energy in order to pollute its environment with furnace smoke and sewage, required substantial spending on food from outside, and chained its occupants to wage employment to pay the high cost of a mortgage. The Ark was the antithesis of this house, offering a comfortable interior climate while generating its own pollution-free energy, and producing fresh fish and vegetables year round. Early greenhouse results indicated that the Ark could produce surplus food and tree seedlings for local markets sufficient to cover its mortgage costs – a projected harvest of 20,000 fish several times per year, 5,000 pounds of high-value produce such as greens, broccoli and tomatoes, and 10,000 to 20,000 tree seedlings.[14] John Todd envisioned that Ark inhabitants, freed from the need to seek wages to pay the high cost of a mortgage and energy bills, would become active participants in the more satisfying work of providing for their own needs.

The budget breakdown shows the final construction cost of the Ark was $173,000 of the overall $354,000 project budget, giving a cost per square foot of $32 for the

5,500 square foot Ark building (including dwelling, greenhouses, labs, and barn).[15] This was about 50 per cent more than the cost of constructing an ordinary house at the time, a modest premium for an experimental building with a research lab and extensive monitoring equipment. In 2016 dollars, this would be $150 per square foot, roughly the cost of an inexpensive custom house.[16] Hammarlund observed that many people refused to believe the actual costs of the Ark, and instead assumed that the full project budget and more would be needed to achieve something similar; in popular imagination the Ark became a half-million dollar house, an almost unimaginable cost to most Islanders.[17] In New Alchemy's vision of the Ark as income-earning food producer, the additional cost of the large commercial greenhouse would be more than repaid by its produce.

Anticipating the interest of tourists, locals, and people around the world, for the summer of 1977 New Alchemy published a mail-ready, six-fold pamphlet describing the Ark, its vision, design, and systems. One part of the mission is "to explore directions for change in the way we live," demonstrating these potentials while acting as "a unique centre for ongoing research." Protecting the research mission was already top of mind, and the location information was accompanied by a firm statement that the Ark was only open to visitors on Sunday afternoons.[18]

At the end of 1977, New Alchemy's *Quarterly Report* described the results of a full year's operation, monitoring, and research. The building-integrated energy systems performed as well as, or better than, expected. A mix of teething pains and accidents afflicted the active solar heating systems, though nothing beyond what would be expected in debugging a new state-of-the-art system.[19] Fortunately the performance of the passive solar energy systems mostly eliminated the need for the active systems. The wood stove, as a responsive source of local heat, played a key role in providing comfort to the inhabitants. The Suntube fish tanks and deep planting beds provided nearly sufficient thermal mass for the greenhouse. The rock storage system provided a small amount of supplemental heat to ensure a narrower temperature range, but the effort needed to construct the rock vault and the high energy demand to operate the fan led the New Alchemists to speculate about modest design adjustments to eliminate the rock storage system altogether.[20]

On the food systems side, the Ark developed best practices in deep soil organic greenhouse agriculture. Early indications of plant performance, vegetable yields, and biological pest control were all positive, and the feasibility of the proposed cash-crop production in mid-winter, when its market value would be highest, was established.[21] The Suntube aquaculture system also offered unanticipated scope. The use of its nutrient-rich water to irrigate and fertilize planting beds inspired the use of

4.09

A COMPARISON OF THE ARK WITH ORTHODOX HOUSING		
CATEGORY	**ARK**	**ORTHODOX HOUSING**
UTILIZES THE SUN *	Source of Heating, Climate, Purification, Food Production and Much In winter Light	Same Interior Light - Often Negative Role Necessitating Air Conditioning
UTILIZES THE WIND	A Source of Electrical Energy from Windmill Wind-Driven Circulation through Composting Toilet	Only Negatively, Increasing Fuel Demands through Infiltration
STORES ENERGY	YES - In Three Systems and Growing	NO
MICRO-CLIMATOLOGICAL SITING	Integral in Design	Rare
WASTE PURIFICATION	YES - Except for Grey Water which is Piped into Leaching Bed	Wastes Untreated and Discharged to Pollute
WASTE UTILIZATION	Purified Wastes are Nutrient Sources or Interior Biological Cycles	NO
FUEL USE	Wood, a Renewable Source as Supplemental Heat	Heavy Use of Gas, Oil or Inefficient Electricity
ENERGY CONSERVING	YES - Also Uses Energy to Serve Sound Systems Functions	NO, or Rarely
ELECTRICITY CONSUMPTION	Almost none as Orthodox House but Electricity Used for Many Productive and Economic Functions	Fairly Heavy Consumer
FOODS	Diverse Foods Cultured Year Round	Not Within - Often Summer Gardens
AGRICULTURAL CROPS	Vegetables, Flowers and Young Trees	NO
AQUACULTURAL PRODUCE	Fish for Market	NO
ECONOMIC UNIT	YES - Viability to be Determined	NO - Financial Burden
OPERATIONAL COST	LOW - Ultimately Equitive as Power	HIGH - Particularly in Fuels and Electricity
INITIAL COST	HIGH - Due to Energy and Biological Components - Uses Larger Amounts of Quality Materials	Moderate
VULNERABILITY TO INFLATION AND SHORTAGES	SLIGHT	SEVERE
IMPROVES CLIMATE AND LOCAL ENVIRONMENT	YES - Locally by Woodlands and More Broadly through Reforestation	RARELY - Most Intensify Weather
TEACHES ABOUT THE LARGER WORKINGS OF NATURE	YES	NO
INCREASES SELF-SUFFICIENCY	YES	Rarely
STIMULATES LOCAL AND REGIONAL SOLUTIONS	Possible	Unlikely

4.10

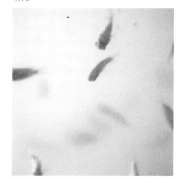

4.09 "A Comparison of the Ark with Orthodox Housing," from the Ark Report of December 1976 (5). John Todd argued that in contrast to "consumptive" orthodox houses, the Ark is an active "producer" of food, energy, and economic sufficiency.
4.10 Close-up of aquaculture in a Suntube solar fish pond, showing Tilapia swimming in dense algae.

the tank's surface water for hydroponic plant cultivation.[22] After the ability to produce tilapia in quantity was established over the first winter, the aquaculture experiments focused on establishing simulation models for solar-algae pond systems rather than on commercial fish production. The Ark also established a successful trial rainbow trout hatchery, producing pan-sized fish in one year. Suntube ponds were linked in a "solar river" that also provided biological polyculture water filtration, using tanks containing a mix of plants, snails, and other cleansing organisms.[23] This cold-water aquaculture complemented New Alchemy's well-established tropical tilapia aquaculture technique.[24]

Over 600 people visited the Ark each Sunday through the summer, and 100-200 each Sunday even into November. Special tours were held for groups and dignitaries on Wednesday afternoons. Bilingual signage was installed to interpret the features and systems.[25] Amory Lovins was impressed by the Ark's integrated ecology:

> The biologically sophisticated Ark project makes manifest our interdependence with the natural world, reintegrating us into it and enhancing our sense of wholeness: a special strength of combined innovation in energy and agricultural systems.[26]

Systems Lessons and Logics

While the Ark's active systems – the billboard of solar panels and water storage, the greenhouse rock storage, and the Hydrowind turbine – dominated its media image, the hearts and minds of the New Alchemy/Solsearch team belonged to the integrated passive solar and biology approaches. Active solar and wind systems served the technology development ambitions of the funding agencies within Environment Canada, but the first year of operation showed that these systems were expensive, complex, and ultimately unnecessary – most vividly during a three day storm in November 1976, when the Ark relied on passive storage and a small amount of wood. In films and magazine articles about life in the Ark, residents Willis and Bergmark downplayed the active systems, and pointed out that most Canadian homes could substantially reduce their energy consumption by simpler means: windbreaks, lots of southern-facing windows with few or none to the north, and highly insulated, airtight walls.[27] A solar design pamphlet was printed in 1977 emphasizing passive approaches, to counter visitors' perceptions that solar energy was costly, complex, and "out of reach."[28] In 1980, when Solsearch summarized their bioshelter experience, they commented that "active solar heat works but is too expensive" and they only cautiously advocated active solar collection for domestic water.[29]

The contrast between active and passive energy approaches was most stark in the case of the Hydrowind turbine. While the solar panels and rock heat storage vaults

4.11 In the family greenhouse, looking up towards the dining room, 1977.
4.12 The Hydrowind turbine, with its equipment shed in the foreground, 1977. New Alchemy made bold promises about the potential of Hydrowind to solve the Island's electricity challenges.
4.13 A tour group in the commercial greenhouse, seen from the Ark kitchen, 1977. Glass separates the variable temperature and humidity of the commercial greenhouse from the climate of the dwelling.

were carefully integrated into the fabric of the Ark, the turbine stood at a distance, connected to the bio-architectural system only by a cable. It was designed in isolation from the Ark design team by several consulting engineers led by New Alchemist Tyrone Cashman.[30] In the *Final Report* it is presented in a separate section from the integrated architecture and biology of the bioshelter. While the Hydrowind turbine was initially conceived to serve the energy needs of the Ark, John Todd's ambitions for it were much bigger: he foresaw an extensive network of turbines connected to the Island's power grid, replacing the existing diesel generators while avoiding the need to connect to New Brunswick's nuclear power station.[31] Such a Hydrowind network would localize power generation, increasing its democratic potential. Its grid-connected approach avoided the need for expensive battery storage typical of standalone windmill and alternative energy systems of the era, anticipating contemporary wind power deployment, while its striking visual presence helped establish wind power in the public imagination. But a Hydrowind network demanded no change in the consumerist lifestyles served by the power; it simply changed the inputs of a business-as-usual system of distribution. A key aspect of Appropriate Technology is lacking – the expectation of "the participation of the people whose interest it is intended to serve."[32] Hydrowind followed an "eco-technical" logic, in which technology is used to reduce environmental impacts, but without the associated social implications.[33]

In contrast, the integrated bio-architectural ecosystem of the Ark proposed a transformed relationship between human environments and nature, in which people were to take an active part in providing for their own needs. Its vision of creative collaboration with nature follows an "eco-social" ethic, which aspires to change social relations between people and their environments.[34] Where Hydrowind offered a one-component fix to an existing power grid, the Ark envisioned an entirely new way of being. Presented together, their incompatible logics became muddled; the "easy" road of Hydrowind power undermined the transformative challenge of the bioshelter. Hydrowind was also disproportionately expensive, accounting for almost a third of the overall Ark budget; this amount was often lumped in to inflate the Ark building costs reported in the media. But far more damaging was the abject failure of Hydrowind to deliver on its promise. The hydraulics and variable-pitch vanes were over-complex and ill-suited to the site conditions. Hydrowind's cost, complexity, and failure to deliver reliable power became a weapon for naysayers to use against the Ark, harming its reputation by association.[35]

4.12

4.13

4.14

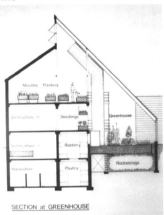

4.15

SECTION at GREENHOUSE

4.16

Deploying the Lessons of the Ark

Ole Hammarlund and his family had returned to Cambridge after the Ark opening, where Solsearch Architects maintained their original office. In early 1977, Solsearch established a Charlottetown office in partnership with local architect Doug Miller, and Bergmark commuted there daily. For the next several years the two architects were in a constant shuttle between offices as they pursued opportunities to apply the Ark principles in other projects and settings. Hammarlund began a long-term personal exploration of the Ark ideas in "Spunky Root," a pole structure cottage hand-built of local and recycled materials across the bay from the Ark, before he moved to the Island permanently in 1979.[36]

Practicing as Solsearch Architects in the USA and as Miller Solsearch in Canada, Bergmark and Hammarlund deployed active building energy and biological systems in several unbuilt designs for larger-scale, Ark-like bioshelters, such as the 1978 B.E.S.S. Bioshelter project in the Bronx, NY.[37] In 1977 they adapted the Ark's passive energy systems for their Conserver One and Conserver Two houses, which featured high insulation and airtightness, low energy consumption, and micro-greenhouses as buffering spaces.[38] Their energy requirements were sufficiently reduced that no furnaces were needed. As in 21st century passive houses, heat was drawn from occupant activities and appliances, supplemented by baseboard distribution from a conventional domestic hot water heater. Conserver One was developed and self-built by Solsearch in the Hillsborough neighbourhood of Charlottetown.[39] IMR commissioned the Conserver Two design, which was built by an Island contractor and sold for a cost comparable to conventional Island houses.[40] IMR and Solsearch sold inexpensive Conserver House blueprints to the public, and several more were built. Solsearch also completed a number of new house designs and renovations with greenhouse additions.[41] The architectural potential of the greenhouse continued to be an inspiration: "The greenhouses in the Arks … are so beautiful that people want to live there rather than in the designated bedrooms. Is it possible to design a greenhouse … comfortable to live in?"[42] In their 1978 "Ark Two" house design, the large greenhouse accommodates living, dining, and kitchen zones, and connects to the bedrooms. A "solar staircase" provides control of light and heat gain better suited to human inhabitants, with a rock vault storing excess heat. Ark Two won a US Housing and Urban Development Solar Design competition, receiving a $5,000 prize and $7,000 towards the cost of building a first example in Sharon, MA.[43] Bergmark's and Hammarlund's subsequent design work, as collaborators and independently, continues to re-imagine architecture as integrated with sustainable energy and the environment.

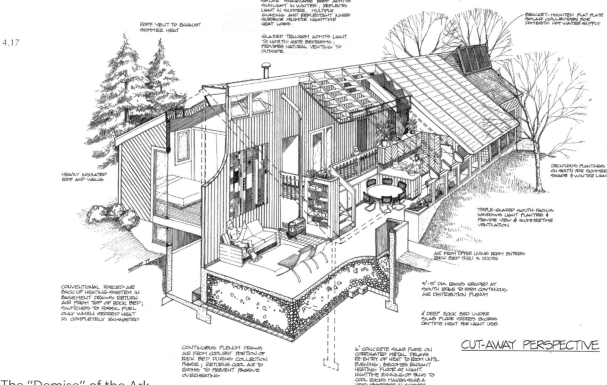

CUT-AWAY PERSPECTIVE

The "Demise" of the Ark

Writing in 1981, E.F. Schumacher's associate George McRobie claimed that the combination of the Ark and the Institute for Man and Resources (IMR) made up "one of the most carefully planned and well structured efforts at energy and food self-sufficiency in existence anywhere in the Western world."[44] Despite such continuing international public support and recognized contributions to research, the Ark project encountered creeping hostility in Island media and political circles. Public perceptions of the Ark began to shift. The demonstration side for visitors remained popular (although the over-zealous enthusiasm of some visitors continued to disrupt the researchers and the Ark family), and international coverage remained positive. But the research side of the Ark's work, and especially its advocacy of new ways of living, was troubled by the cultural politics of regional belonging. According to an increasing number of media accounts and conservative politicians, the New Alchemists at the Ark were "come-from-aways," despite the fact that several had settled on the island for a good duration.[45] Settled more than an hour outside Charlottetown, running an experiment in self-sufficient living, they interacted mostly with the local community and with their international counterparts at

4.14 Spunky Root cottage, Launching, PE, Hammarlund & Lips, 1977 – ongoing. Construction view, 1979. The upper bedroom window framed a view of the Ark across the bay.
4.15 The B.E.S.S. Bioshelter, Bronx, NY, cross-section showing layers of agricultural production. Solsearch Architects, ink on mylar, 1978.
4.16 Conserver Two House, Charlottetown, PE, showing the small greenhouse on the south side. Solsearch Architects, 1979.
4.17 "Low Energy House Perspective View," Ark Two Low Energy House. Solsearch Architects, ink and pencil on tracing paper, 1978.

4.18

Cape Cod and beyond. Their profile "in town" was low. While the nationally-focused CBC in Charlottetown was generally supportive, coverage in the Charlottetown *Guardian* newspaper became increasingly sceptical; Montague's *Eastern Graphic* newspaper was openly hostile right from the opening day.[46]

During the construction and living experiment era of the Ark, the IMR was pursuing related technology transfer efforts. It also completed various demonstration projects on the Island at scales ranging from individual home energy retrofits to a combined heat and power biomass plant.[47] IMR Director Andy Wells had been prominent in drawing the New Alchemists to the Island to build the Ark. This, combined with many overlapping areas of interest, meant that the New Alchemists, the Ark, and the IMR were closely linked – and often confused – in the public mind. The IMR was also criticized for promoting ideas "from away." Although it was based "in town" and run by Islanders, it brought international characters such as Amory Lovins and George McRobie to Energy Days events, where they promoted alternative ideas.[48] When the IMR encouraged Islanders to change their energy habits and expectations, the Charlottetown news media were similarly unenthusiastic. These various missions, people, and projects were easily muddled in the public mind, and both credit and criticism were easily misplaced.

The future of the New Alchemy Institute on the Island was threatened almost from the start by the unexpected withdrawal of support from Environment Canada, for the Ark and for the alternative approaches it embodied. Advanced Concepts Centre staff involved in the Ark's development had been forbidden from attending the opening in 1976, and Environment Canada had no official presence at the event.[49] By the end of 1977 the Advanced Concepts Centre had shifted focus to international eco-development policy, and its renewable energy experts dispersed to EMR and the National Research Council. According to Bruce McCallum, the deputy ministers had re-asserted territoriality within the federal bureaucracy, ending the operation of the informal "eco-network."[50] This renewed territoriality ended the Ark's financial independence. The New Alchemy Institute had understood that upon completion of the Ark in 1976, they would receive a direct two-year federal-provincial research grant of $351,000 through Environment Canada.[51] Presented in June 1977 under the title "The Ark Project," New Alchemy developed a detailed plan of work, budget, and staffing, articulated in eight sub-projects ranging from "Management & Scientific Direction" through "Information & Outreach." New Alchemy planned to continue monitoring the systems, undertake adjustments and design changes identified through the first year, and install a sophisticated microcomputer to monitor and model the overall "energetics" of the Ark.

4.18 The south side of the Ark, Summer 1977. Outdoor vegetable gardens complemented greenhouse production.

This would go beyond monitoring individual systems to analyse the complex energy flows throughout the Ark's integrated physical and biological systems, providing key design data to future architects and biological designers.[52]

Environment Canada's promised funds were provided instead via a three-year, $6 million Canada-PEI "Agreement on Renewable Energy Development" announced in early 1977, jointly funded with Energy, Mines and Resources. This contract was to be managed by the IMR, and the IMR would in turn pay the New Alchemy Institute to run the demonstration and research activities at the Ark. The amount to flow to New Alchemy was much less than they were originally promised, and neither the energetics research nor the systems improvements were supported. At this time, the province had still not transferred the Spry Point site to the New Alchemists, who were feeling increasingly vulnerable. Even the name of the funding program was a blow, implying that the Ark's food systems research was not relevant. And it was the IMR, their natural ally on the Island, that would be the instrument of New Alchemy's marginalization. According to Nancy Willis,

> By the end of the year we pretty well knew what we needed to know, so the project was almost obsolete for us at that time. In a meeting with the federal government and the province, we were told that funds would only funnel through one stream, and that funding stream was going to be the IMR. They offered us the option of living there and operating it – they didn't say as a tourism site, but that's what it was. We were *so* not interested in that.[53]

The restructured funding arrangement and the IMR's plans for the future of the Ark were unappealing to the New Alchemists. 1977 was a year of bickering over research direction and programs at the Ark, and especially about inadequate management (in the minds of IMR) of what the New Alchemists considered their inadequate allocation of funds.[54] The living experiment came to an end in March 1978 when the New Alchemy Institute transferred the Ark to the IMR and the Ark family moved out.[55] IMR adopted the title "The Ark Project" from the New Alchemists' proposal but little else. IMR's operating plan emphasized the demonstration function of the Ark, recognizing its popularity with the public and its growing value as a tourist destination.[56] Later in 1978 Solsearch designed a conversion of the living room into an orientation theatre for visitors.[57] No longer a "living experiment," the Ark was now free to serve primarily as a public demonstration project, and visitor numbers increased to many hundreds per week in the next few summers.[58] Willis stayed on, now as Director of the Ark Project, until the autumn of 1978, when IMR hired its own Director, Ken McKay.[59] Under IMR the energy systems monitoring and food systems research continued, with New Alchemists Willis and Linda Gilkeson retained to run the greenhouse program, but the energy systems changes were rejected. Solsearch continued to work at the site, collaborating with IMR on a feasibility study of a greenhouse design using mud as heat storage; a prototype was begun on the Ark site.[60] For Willis, the commitment to fulfilling the New Alchemists' vision on the Island continued long after she departed the Spry Point site. She has since pursued a career in journalism with the CBC, the Charlottetown *Guardian*, and other outlets, giving a voice on the Island to issues of environmental and social justice, and promoting ecologically-based agricultural practices. Bergmark and Hammarlund have also remained active in shaping the Island's physical and cultural environment, with Solsearch Architects becoming Bergmark and Hammarlund Architects, and eventually combining forces with architects George Guimond and Larry Jones to form BGHJ Architects.

4.19

The Ark after New Alchemy

After New Alchemy's departure, the Ark carried on. A two-day technical review meeting was convened in November 1978, led by Robert Durie and including 14 specialists "selected to provide expertise which covered the scope of elements which together made up this unique project."[61] Durie, John Todd, and Andy Wells were joined by federal civil servants, academics, an architect, and two independent policy analysts. Durie's overview indicates that there were no fundamental technical failures identified (other than the Hydrowind), and was at pains to point out the importance of the "integrated nature of the Ark." According to the technical review,

> The Ark expressed an evolving image of "environment." Environmental action in the late 1960s and early 1970s had concentrated on defensive measures such as pollution control, but to an increasing degree the issue was seen as a broader concern for … initiatives which would assure a secure, quality environment for the future[….] The Ark was a project compatible with this shifting awareness of the nature of environmental issues.[62]

The main conclusion of the review was that the Ark should shift away from the demonstration focus imposed by IMR in early 1978, to a research focus. While acknowledging that the Ark's "appeal to imagination, creativity, and concern of Canadians and people world wide" was the basis of its success, the review panel felt that the symbolic dimension of the Ark – the image of the self-sufficient family home – was also the major source of scepticism and criticism. The gambit was to pre-empt this critique by making clear that the Ark was merely researching the "concept" of self-sufficiency; but in the very next paragraph the report also noted the "minor point" that the Ark "is neither well situated nor suitable for a general research role."[63]

Initial research results seemed to support the refocus. The wind power research was shifted to the new Atlantic Wind Test Centre at North Cape, though several windmills remained at Spry Point. After troubleshooting the controls, the active solar energy systems performed to expectations, but the passive solar and wood heating systems remained the focus of technology-transfer efforts to Island houses.[64] Natural pest management strategies were refined and popularized, along with other best practices for solar greenhouse production. Aquaculture was expanded to include rainbow and speckled trout and Atlantic salmon, with the solar river system expanded to use bacteria, plants, and snails for water filtration. Hydroponics on the Suntube surfaces was yielding lettuce, chard, tomatoes, and broccoli. Including the soil-based beds, the Ark greenhouse was producing two high-value vegetable harvests and one major fish harvest per year, at a total energy cost of 30 cents per square foot per year (compared to $1-$2 per square foot per year for Ontario's fossil fuelled greenhouses of the day). Results and best practices from the food and energy systems were published in conference papers, IMR reports, and popular media. And 5,000 visitors per year continued to tour the Ark.[65]

But the tenor of governmental attitudes towards the Ark did not bode well for its future. The muddle of reputations and perceptions between the IMR and the Ark only worsened with the new arrangements. Reactionary critics now had a single, clear target for their scorn. IMR was a provincial Liberal government project under the auspices of Premier Alex Campbell who, perhaps sensing the coming conservative winds, stepped down as leader in 1978. Angus McLean's Progressive Conservatives won the 1979 provincial election, and though IMR's Wells had believed his institute to be an arm's-length agency above politics, the new government's indifference and hostility to its goals and programs became clear.[66] From its Charlottetown vantage point, IMR began to perceive the Ark as a risk to its own future. Despite the positive technical review report, Environment Canada drastically cut its annual funding to the Ark in July 1979. EMR, their funding partner in the Canada-PEI agreement, protested, citing the likely result as the closure of the Ark and the loss of its "local, national, and international impact." Funding was restored, but only for 1979.[67] The 1980 extension of the Canada-PEI agreement on renewable energy development made no reference nor funding allocation to the Ark or its programs; additionally, the IMR itself was cut out of the overall contract management role for the agreement, and instead had to compete for individual contracts, substantially reducing its base funding.[68] IMR's Charlottetown-based Ark staff felt that commuting to Spry Point was an unnecessary burden, while diminishing attention to the energy systems left the Ark vulnerable to charges of research obsolescence.

4.19 "The Ark" coffee mug, from the era under the direction of the Institute for Man and Resources. IMR commissioned the logo from noted Island graphic designer Marc Gallant.

4.20 "Province of Prince Edward Island: Request for Proposals for the Ark – Spry Point." Display ad 32, *Globe and Mail*, 31 March 1982, B6.
4.21 "Spry Point Co-op Ark Project" aerial perspective. Drawing by David Bergmark, Bergmark & Hammarlund Architects, pencil on tracing paper, 1988. The existing building (right) was altered to house a restaurant and guest rooms. An unbuilt addition with more guest rooms (left) evoked the massing of the Ark.

On January 23, 1981, Andy Wells regretfully notified the federal and provincial governments that the Ark would be handed back to their care. A draft IMR Newsletter announcing this decision expressed the hope that the "Ark's owners" would continue its seasonal operation as a demonstration centre, and concluded with the mailing addresses of the two Ministers of the Environment and a suggestion that the public write to demand continued support.[69] PEI Energy Minister Barry Clark moved quickly to head this off. In a January 27 interview on CBC television, he claimed to be surprised by the IMR announcement and questioned the validity of the Ark research, saying

> certainly there was a negative feeling about the project … I feel that the Ark in many ways failed to meet the expectations that Islanders had for it …. Many people 'come from away' thought it was the greatest thing … but I don't think we [in PEI] have seen very much benefit from it.[70]

In this attack, the Minister set out the narrative that would come to define the Ark's legacy in Charlottetown government circles: that it was a failure, its research not valid, its lessons not relevant to the Island, and that the Ark was somehow a trick that outsiders had played on a simple local folk.[71] News stories on and off the Island about the Ark's imminent closure and its later life picked up the premise that the local Islanders had always resented the "arrogant incomers" and their odd ways; the legacy of the Ark's important experiments in Appropriate Technology were falsely dismissed as having "failed miserably."[72]

Soon the province, and by extension the federal government, entirely severed involvement with the Ark. In March 1982, the province placed notices in newspapers across Canada that "interested parties are invited to submit proposals for their use of the Ark (New Alchemy Institute buildings and land), Spry Point, Prince Edward Island."[73] Solsearch Architects submitted a minimalist strategy to create an "Ark Park" combining ecology and camping. The centrepiece would be "the Ark, once the flagship of Canada's alternative energy efforts, … now retired to become an object of history."[74] Solsearch's perspective was that the end of its research function meant the Ark could now be freed to meet the pent-up demand for public tours, augmented by educational programs and workshops. The continuing high profile and positive reception of the Ark outside PEI could help create a market for eco-tourism. However, given the hostility of the Conservative government to the Ark, a proposal celebrating its historic legacy did not find favour. Richard Davis, described in Island news reports as a "secretive" fish hatchery operator from Toronto, repurposed New Alchemy's solar aquaculture system, but abandoned the other systems.[75] This was the first of a series of picaresque afterlives eventually leading to the Ark's demolition in 1999. For John Todd, the international acclaim for the Ark showed that "good ideas, cast in a beautiful and simple way, could have a big effect," while its quick demise indicated that such good ideas may incite unexpected reactionary counterforces in society. While models and demonstrations such as the Ark might move imaginations, Todd felt they were not sufficient by themselves to bring about societal change.[76]

The Ark in the Spry Point Community

While many media reports played up the claim that the Ark was an alien intrusion resented by the local community, the actual experience indicates quite the opposite. From the initial hospitality extended to the New Alchemists, the intense commitment of local builders through the construction period, the rallying of Spry Point in the final push, and community participation in the opening day events, it is clear that the New Alchemists and their Ark were welcomed and accepted in the community. This sense of welcome transformed their concept of the relationship between the Ark and its setting. The Habitat '76 competition proposal described the PEI Ark as a kind of "spaceship" containing a "capsule environment," suggesting that coming to the Island was a voyage

4.21

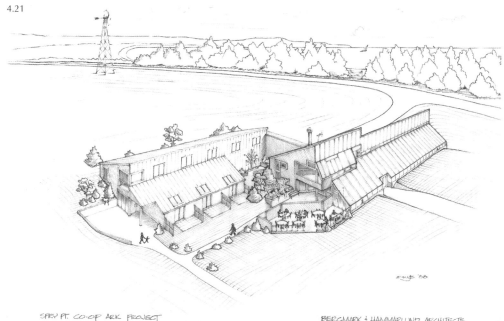

SPRY PT. CO-OP ARK PROJECT   BERGMARK & HAMMARLUND ARCHITECTS

to a hostile environment.[77] This space age, almost science fictional understanding was reinforced by the proposal narrative's insistence on autonomy; by its claim that the Ark would produce all food, satisfy all energy needs, and manage all wastes of its family of four; and in the plan for various New Alchemy families to take turns spending a "mission" living in the Ark. In fact, they had created a self-sufficient (but not autonomous) household and ecosystem, situated in a context of productive small farms which operated on traditional principles relevant to New Alchemy's own agricultural ideals. Working with the community through the construction period and the living experiment, the New Alchemists came to understand the Ark as an integrated part of the ongoing agricultural life of the Island. Ark food systems connected to the economic life of the Island in a reciprocal exchange of goods, similar to the grid-interconnection of the Ark's Hydrowind-based power system. The Ark provided the local markets with low-cost protein in the form of tilapia, and with fresh vegetables in winter when imports were pricey and poor quality. John Todd reported:

> On Prince Edward Island, where food tastes are not generally sophisticated, the demand for produce from the Ark has outstripped our supplies. Even if the Ark were altered from an experimental to a production facility, we could not meet the demand in the rural area where the Institute is situated. A large number of bioshelters producing year-round foods would have ready access to local outlets as such a market is not easily saturated.[78]

Responding to the Spry Point hospitality, the "spaceship" Ark became a "local producer" Ark, its captive ecosystem released to participate in the local economy and community. Rather than being a fully autonomous bioshelter, it became a net producer of food and energy for the local economy, drawing traditional goods and services from the community while offering its own produce to market. Along the way, its innovative inhabitants introduced new ideas about food, and fresh ingredients year-round, to local diets. The exchange was cultural as well as economic.

Spry Point's affection for "our Ark" continued long after the departure of the New Alchemists and Solsearch. When the fish hatchery abandoned the building in 1986, the people of Spry Point formed a cooperative to take back the Ark; after two years of uncertainty, the co-op took on the lease in 1988.[79] Bergmark and Hammarlund designed a renovation to convert the Ark to an Inn, with eight guest rooms along the north side of the greenhouse; their design for an additional wing of guest rooms remained unbuilt. A 60-seat restaurant occupied the greenhouse, enjoying a remnant of the intimacy with nature that moved so many early Ark visitors. Much of the active New Alchemy systems had been removed or abandoned, but the grapevine planted by Nancy Willis in 1977 dominated the greenhouse, evidence of the continued effectiveness of the passive solar system.[80] Some systems were restored as part of an effort to present the history of the Ark's lifestyle experiment to a new generation. Finally opened in 1990, the co-op ran the "Spry Point Ark" until 1997, when it ran into difficulties borrowing money for maintenance and upgrades. They had requested title to the property from the province to allow them to secure a mortgage, but instead the government chose to put the site to sale by tender. The Spry Point group made a proposal, but the high bidder was American-based tourism developer David Wilmer.

The people of Spry Point made an emotional claim to the Ark as having been a source of pride, employment, and economic development from the time it was first created, and argued that they were in the best position to build on its international reputation as an alternative lifestyle experiment.[81] Their pleas were of no avail. The Ark was demolished to its foundations in 1999 and replaced by the Inn at Spry Point, a twee, neo-traditional boutique resort with 15 rooms and a restaurant. At the Inn's opening in 2000, the news coverage referred to the hope that the new-old Inn would overcome the Ark's "international notoriety" to draw tourists to eastern PEI.[82] The forward-looking Ark was replaced by a backward-looking exercise in nostalgia, in an act of cultural erasure welcomed by a provincial government afraid of embracing its progressive recent past, preferring instead an inn to serve the homely myths of an "innocent" pre-modern island of family farms. Lucy Maud Montgomery's Anne Shirley might test the edges of propriety, but ultimately she abides by the status quo. Nostalgia is the preferred mode of contemporary tourism in Atlantic Canada, closely aligned with hedonistic consumerism in the form of golfing and four-star restaurants. Solsearch and New Alchemy, incomers hoping to support the local community by demonstrating a self-sufficient lifestyle, were supplanted by high-end tourists, incomers expecting to be catered to by local people precariously employed in seasonal work.

Right up to its end, the Ark building witnessed the potential of creative collaboration involving official culture, the counterculture, and local cultures. In the spirit of the New Alchemists' mentor Margaret Mead, it showed that the actions of a small group of determined people can effect lasting change in the world and – despite the seemingly unstoppable forces of globalization and consumerism – real people in real places can assert control over the technologies of their lives by providing for their food and energy needs in ways that are democratic and local.[83] Demolition removed any remaining physical evidence that might counter the failure narrative that had become associated with the Ark. Such destruction of buildings is in part a destruction of memory, which, as George Orwell pointed out, is a tactic to control the direction of the present and future.

4.22

4.23

4.22 The Ark for Prince Edward Island, aerial view, 1976.
4.23 The Inn at Spry Point, aerial view. Guimond + Associates Architects, 2000. The Inn occupies the footprint of the Ark, which was demolished in 1999.

4.24

As evidence of a road not taken, the Ark was now erased for the convenience of a neo-liberal tourism-based economy.[84]

Visionary Architecture, Dreams of Appropriate Technology

> In recent years architects have begun to design energy conserving buildings yet the overall function of buildings in modern societies is ignored. … The Ark is one of the first synthetically framed explorations of a new direction for human habitations. … It begins to redefine how humans might live in Canada. The Ark is in no way an end point, but an early investigation of a viable new direction.
> - New Alchemy Institute 1976[85]

Many assessments of the Ark are based on a fundamental misconception of its purpose. Most buildings are answers offered by their designers to well-understood needs and conventional intentions, using well-established materials and techniques. As John Todd pointed out, the Ark was never intended as an answer, but rather was offered as a question about the role of buildings in transforming the way people live on Earth. Its materials and systems were likewise questions, and the story of the design process shows how knowledge emerged through the learning-by-doing approach of New Alchemy and Solsearch. Dismissing the Ark because some systems did not succeed initially misses the point of experimentation entirely, which seeks proof both positive and negative. With the demise of the Ark, its explorations were continued on PEI and Cape Cod, and its approaches were adopted elsewhere.

The Ark deployed experimental technologies and design approaches that have become emblems of sustainable design today. Much "green architecture" of the 1970s and even today is designed to mitigate the negative impacts of buildings, but it accepts without question the consumer lifestyle – its highest goal is harm-reduction.[86] What set the Ark apart from such "green architecture" was its ambition to change the basis of humanity's relationship with the environment. John Todd believed that the Ark systems "integrated with and dependent upon living systems should have the … effect [of] teaching us how the world works. Their inhabitants conceivably might become better stewards of the earth."[87]

Visionary projects are a recurring theme in architectural history, offering radical speculations about new ways of configuring space, new approaches to structure and form, new experiences, and new effects. Whether the medieval plan for an ideal monastery of St. Gall, Switzerland, Étienne-Louis Boullée's Cenotaph for Newton in revolutionary France, the Constructivist fantasies of the Russian Revolution, or the "Walking Cities" of Archigram in the 1960s, visionary architecture has for the most

4.24 Nancy Willis and Josh Smith tending to the deep soil planting beds in the Commercial Greenhouse, 1977.

part been paper architecture, expressed in drawings and models. These images garnish the study of architectural history, sometimes as the sources for later buildings, other times counterfactual hints of paths not taken. Only slowly and by small increments do such visions find their way into actual buildings.[88] Paper architecture also dominates Appropriate Technology publications: examples include Buckminster Fuller's Manhattan dome, the "Bioshelter" illustrations of Chahroudi and Wellesley-Miller, and the images of self-sufficient city blocks in Peter Harper and Godfrey Boyle's *Radical Technology*.[89]

Remarkably, the Ark was a visionary project that was actually built, and consequently available for both inspiration and study. The building's materials and systems were, like the concept of the Ark, posed as questions rather than solutions. Its design process incorporated the knowledge acquired through the learning-by-doing approach of New Alchemy and Solsearch: the initial vision was deeply researched, and the design was then developed by extensive and creative collaboration over several iterations, including trials of materials and systems. Once it was built and its energy, food, and waste systems were installed and operating, the Ark's performance was carefully monitored for more than a year, and the results were shared in official and popular venues. Following the demise of the Ark, its explorations into both the means and the ends of buildings were continued on Cape Cod and elsewhere, and its lessons were picked up and carried forward by others around the world. The "fact" of the Ark was crucial; because the Ark existed in a real, material form, the Ark vision gained plausibility and potency.

Over its short life, the Ark received tens of thousands of visitors. Many hundred thousands more around the world experienced it through news reports, film, and television. The Ark empowered people to imagine a very different future world, one of self-sufficiency, of "living lightly on the earth," free from the twin tyrannies of fossil fuels and nuclear energy. Just as attractive was the intimate dream of enjoying winter while tending plants in a sunny greenhouse. The mix of planting beds and fish tanks, set in the wood and glass Ark with views to the land and sea beyond, offered a dream of sun-filled, spacious, and green sufficiency.

Young people saw the Ark in the context of the counterculture, as a chance to take direct action in making a better world. Appropriate Technology activists saw it as a focus for their emerging repertoire of freely shared, people-oriented tools for building a convivial future. Politicians and government officials used the Ark as a lens to look outside their usual circles of expertise to find innovative policies and practices to face down a global environmental and energy crisis. Locals were curious about what the incomers were up to with government money, but also willing to help out their

4.25 Winter view of the Ark for PEI from the southwest, ca. Winter 1977. Very little snow accumulated on the greenhouse roof, while plentiful sunlight reached the "billboard" of solar collectors, both directly and by reflection off the snow-covered ground.

new neighbours and even borrow some of their ideas. Richard Thomas, a freelance broadcaster from Ontario, visited the Ark during a February 1977 blizzard:

> What I'm talking about is how the people I represent, the people I live with, would look at this. It's snowing outside, it's cold, the wind is howling somewhere up near 90 kilometres an hour, there's snow accumulating on [the greenhouse] and falling off every so often, but as far as I know there's a little wood burning over there, there's 1800 square feet, and there's flowers growing. They want it – how long are they going to have to wait?[90]

"How long" indeed. Four decades after Pierre Trudeau spoke of a future of "living lightly on the earth," humanity faces many of the same environmental challenges addressed by the PEI Ark, though now with a greater sense of urgency, a reduced sense of individual and community agency to tackle them, and an expectation of diminished future lifestyles and human possibilities.

Almost twenty years after its demolition, the Ark remains a touchstone for many, a memory of a vision of a compelling, sustainable future. The Ark's ecological architecture offers a spirit of critical hope, embodying the adventure of creative collaboration between science and society, and among governments, communities, and individuals. The story of the Ark for Prince Edward Island is the story of a compelling road not (yet) taken, offering lessons and inspiration for meeting the environmental challenges of the 21st century. It is a potent reminder of the dream, not yet realized but still within reach, of how we might live in harmony and collaboration with the earth's ecosystems.

4.26

4.26 Modern Architecture meets Old Technology: The Ark for PEI viewed from the west with an old pole wagon in the foreground, Fall 1976.
4.27 "Section @ Dwelling & Mechanical Space," Ark for PEI presentation drawing, scale 1 inch = 4 feet. Solsearch Architects, ink on mylar, dated October 1975 (actual date Fall 1976). The interwoven spaces and systems include (left) the kitchen greenhouse with small "Suntube" solar fish ponds, open to the kitchen/dining area. The domestic hot water tank in the attic connects to the sloped solar panels. Basement water tanks store heat from the vertical "billboard" of solar collectors; in front is the Clivus Multrum composting chamber.

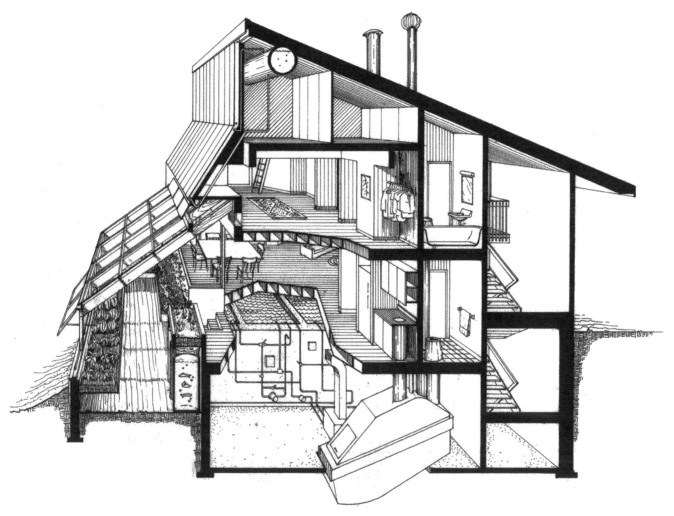

SECTION @ DWELLING & MECHANICAL SPACE

5.01

Coda: The Cape Cod Ark

5

In the spring of 1975, in the midst of intense design work for the PEI Ark, private donors John and Edith Muma provided funds to build an Ark bioshelter at New Alchemy's farm/research institute near Woods Hole. This "Cape Cod Ark" would fulfill the desire for a temperate bioshelter to complement the Prince Edward Island and Costa Rica experiments, but would also severely test the capacity of the New Alchemists. As Nancy Jack Todd later wrote, "not even Noah was cavalier enough to attempt to launch two Arks at once and his backing was fairly solid."[1] Solsearch Architects took on this design as well. Although their designs were done in parallel, there were significant differences in climate, funding, and purpose that led to two distinctly different Ark designs. The Cape Cod Ark construction budget, at $30,000, was less than one-quarter of that for the PEI Ark, and its winter climate much less harsh. There was no dwelling component, and the greenhouse was conceived as a temporary experimental building, expanding on the lessons and general configuration of the Six-Pack.[2]

The Cape Cod Ark was organized in three zones, with cylindrical "Suntube" aquaculture tanks to the west; a large central volume with in-ground rectangular fish tanks and planting beds above a large rock heat storage vault; and equipment storage to the east.[3] Vegetable beds were planted directly in the ground at the lowest level on the south side, with terraced beds to the north for perennial crops and fruit and nut trees. Insulated perimeter concrete retaining walls improved passive earth heat storage. Deep planting beds and aquaculture tanks also served as passive solar heating storage and transfer. There were no active solar collector panels. A fan harvested greenhouse air from the high point, drawing it through a rock storage vault and out to a duct below the planting bench along the south wall, creating a thermal flywheel similar to that of the PEI Ark greenhouse. A vertical axis wind turbine provided power for the fans and pumps. Hung from the roof, an "observation and monitoring" platform became a regular hangout space, and an occasional sleeping space, evidence of the discovery of the greenhouse space as just a great place to "be."

The north side of the Ark was nestled into an earth bank for insulation, with a highly insulated roof sloping directly up from grade. The roof's angle and gloss white interior surface helped to reflect winter light. Learning from the first winter's snow accumulation

5.01 The Cape Cod Ark, New Alchemy Institute, Woods Hole, MA, designed by Solsearch Architects and the New Alchemy Institute, 1975-76. Interior view looking towards the east showing the observation platform above the terraced planters, 1977.

5.02

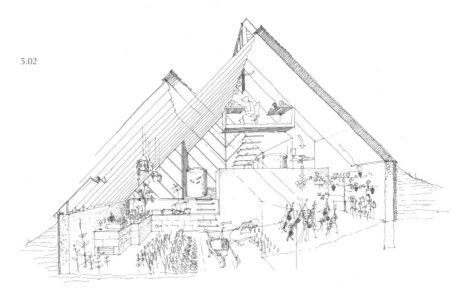

5.03

on the Six-Pack's Kalwall vaults, the greenhouse roof vaults were designed with self-clearing snow slides between the joists, with two layers of Kalwall enclosing a 1-inch air space for insulation.[4] The roof joists supporting the vaults were long 2x2 wood members with a cable-braced king post at mid-span, an effort to minimize the structure and its shadows. End walls repeated the Six-Pack tree branch motif of diagonal wood studs and Kalwall panels. Rippled translucent surfaces and the extreme lightness of construction lent the Cape Cod Ark a 1970s science fiction image, suitable for a space station or extra-terrestrial colony.

In January and February 1976, Ole Hammarlund led the construction team of a hired carpenter and New Alchemy volunteers. Construction of the Cape Cod Ark was, like the Six-Pack, mostly improvised using sketches and hands-on mock-ups, with documentary drawings made after completion.[5] A modest opening ceremony was held on August 11, 1976, a few weeks before the corresponding event on PEI.[6] Reports on its performance and the yields of plants and fish were printed regularly in the *Journal*, culminating in an extensive assessment in issue number 6 (1980), with analysis and comments from New Alchemists and Solsearch on design changes to consider for future Arks.[7] The thoroughness of the review makes the absence of similar long term monitoring and assessment of the PEI Ark all the more disappointing. Though it was expected to last just a few years, the Cape Cod Ark operated in its intended form until 1992. In 1998, New Alchemists Earle Barnhart and Hilde Maingay renewed the Ark and added a dwelling when the site became a co-housing community.[8]

5.02 "Interior Perspective," Cape Cod Ark. Drawing by Ole Hammarlund, Solsearch Architects, ink on mylar, 15 January 1976.
5.03 Cape Cod Ark, exterior view from the southwest, winter 1976.

My Father's Ark

Lukas Bergmark

"An albatross around my neck," is how my father David refers to the PEI Ark, his first major architecture work. Whether he means it as a glib cliché or an intentional reference to the Coleridge ballad, the albatross motif speaks to a feeling of ambivalence about the project. During our childhood, our father did not speak in depth about the PEI Ark. To my siblings and me, it was puzzling that this project was for my father both a source of pride and bitterness. Now, as a recent architecture graduate myself, revisiting the history of the PEI Ark, I have begun to understand David the architect's complex relationship to the Ark and how it has shadowed his life and career.

As Solsearch Architects, David and his partner Ole Hammarlund arrived on Prince Edward Island in 1975 to construct the PEI Ark under the patronage of the New Alchemy Institute. David saw the Island as an untapped sanctuary ready to host a model for a new sustainable society, inspired by this prototype for a self-sustaining building. In the two years he spent building the Ark, David decided that the Island was a place he wanted to stay – lucky for me, as this was where he met my mother Anne Nicholson and started our family.

The PEI Ark successfully exemplified many simple (and a few complex) design solutions to the consumption-driven norms of human dwelling. As Prime Minister Pierre Elliot Trudeau had attested at the Ark's opening, a viable model for "living lightly on the earth" was revealed in the PEI Ark. David and Ole's architecture set a hallmark for sustainable design practice. So why didn't things change for the better? Why didn't people wholeheartedly adopt this new, more sustainable way of living? Had the architects failed to design a building coherent to the general public?

6.01a

6.01b

6.01a "Instamatic" photographs of the Ark's opening taken by David Bergmark's parents. Nancy Willis and David Bergmark in the commercial greenhouse during the official tour.
6.01b David's mother Janet Bergmark beside the open sliding door at the east end of the commercial greenhouse.

Almost before it had begun, the PEI Ark moment was over. After the initial excitement for the Ark and its mission had died down, cheap oil had returned with the end of the OPEC embargo, Islanders had elected a Conservative government in place of the Liberals, and David and Ole's sustainable building had failed to spark change in Island society. These conservative trends made it difficult for David and Ole's practice to pursue sustainable architecture and effect environmentally friendly change on the Island.

To make matters worse, when the Ark was decommissioned in 1981, difficult market conditions on the Island compelled their practice to compete for projects to redesign the unwanted facility. As the original architects, David and Ole were uniquely positioned to win such projects. In the 1980s, they designed an awkward conversion of the Ark into an inn and bed & breakfast. After periods of abandonment the Ark was sold by the province in 1998, and in the same year David and Ole joined forces with two other Island architectural firms to form BGHJ Architects. A member of the new practice secured the commission for a new building at Spry Point, leveraging David's and Ole's relationship with the once renowned Ark. In what was a bittersweet professional moment, the new firm executed the final deathblow to the PEI Ark by replacing it with its literal antithesis, a garish, eclectically styled hotel catering to the leisure class.

I failed to grasp the particular irony of this final destruction of the Ark until I entered practice myself. A life in architecture seems to inevitably involve a struggle between one's architectural ideals and one's ability to feed one's family.

My impression, as a son and young architect, is that my father is proud of the Ark, while also viewing it as a colossal failure. I would argue that the "failure" of the PEI Ark is not due to the Ark's architecture – which can objectively be considered successful, given that the building effectively "worked" as intended – but rather due to the geo-political and economic contexts in which it was situated. Although he acknowledges this hostile social context, my father ultimately feels personal responsibility for the PEI Ark's lack of popular adoption, and for its eventual destruction, I believe.

As an architect, I expect that this comprehensive documentation of an important building now lost will also uncover the effects of the PEI Ark, from subtle to profound, on Island society, and on the sustainable design movement at large. As the architect's son, I hope this process will allow the story of the PEI Ark to stand by itself, contradictory and unresolved as ever, but no longer my father's burden to carry:

And from my [father's] neck so free
The Albatross fell off, and sank
Like lead into the sea.

6.02 David Bergmark with the reconstructed Ark systems model, 2017.
6.03 Ole Hammarlund and David Bergmark at work reconstructing the Ark systems model, December 2015.

Afterword

Kevin Rice

In my first media interview as director of the Confederation Centre Art Gallery in 2009, I hoped I would be able to reflect on some of the pressing environmental concerns being addressed by artists in our exhibition program. Little did I know that *"Living lightly on the earth:" building an Ark for Prince Edward Island, 1974-76* would in many ways be the fullest expression of that intent as it connected so directly to this place, this island in the Gulf of Saint Lawrence, and to growing international awareness and recognition of the urgent need to factor climate change and sustainability, on both micro and macro levels, into our lives.

I was quite excited when Steven Mannell proposed this project in 2014. We would be producing an exhibition about this important architectural project, one that helped bring PEI international acclaim for environmental leadership in the 1970s, yet was no longer widely known here in Prince Edward Island. I felt it was very relevant and that many of our gallery visitors, from seniors to students, for whom the issues of renewable energy and sustainability are important, would appreciate and enjoy a look back.

This exhibition marks the 40th anniversary of the opening of the Ark bioshelter, and, remarkably, many of the people involved at the beginning remain on the Island. Ole Hammarlund is a neighbor and regular visitor to the Art Gallery along with his wife Karen Lips. In the last year, I have happily had many interesting conversations with David Bergmark about this project. While I was aware of their significant roles as the architects of the Ark, I learned through this project that another neighbour, Nancy Willis, who I know of as a committed environmentalist, had lived in the Ark in that first year of operation. The photographs she loaned to this project were very helpful in animating and humanizing the exhibition. I vividly recall Nancy taking the podium at the opening reception; her enthusiasm reminded many younger people that they can make a difference – just as the young Arkies did through collaborations at Spry Point.

Hilde Maingay, one of the founders of the New Alchemy Institute, also gave impromptu remarks at the opening, albeit from a less hopeful point of view. Nevertheless, Hilde's lifelong commitment to sustainable living and her passion for the environment were crystal clear. There was a remarkably genuine level of interest in the project we were revisiting – this leap of imagination and creation towards the ideals of sustainable living still resonates.

I wish to acknowledge and thank the outstanding work of exhibition curator and author Steven Mannell, and his small team of assistants; BGHJ Architects, whose collaboration on this project was critical, as were the loans of many beautiful architectural drawings of the Ark; and to our exhibition sponsors, Veresen/PEI Energy Systems, and the Architects Association of Prince Edward Island, whose support is both helpful and encouraging. My sincere thanks go to the dedicated Gallery staff, and to Centre marketing and development colleagues for their professional contributions to all aspects of the exhibition. The support of the Canada Council for the Arts was critical to the production and curation of this exhibition. While we do plan to tour this important show in upcoming years, we also recognize that exhibitions are by nature ephemeral, so we are fortunate to again collaborate on a publication by Dalhousie Architectural Press to further disseminate the story of the Ark at Spry Point, PEI within their Canadian Modern series.

7.01

7.01 General view of the exhibition at the Confederation Centre Art Gallery, October 2016.
7.02a Gallery visitors with an enlargement of the Solsearch Architects sectional perspective drawing of the Ark barn and commercial greenhouse.
7.02b Model of the final Ark for PEI building and site design, scale 1 inch = 8 feet.
7.02c Model of the Ark for PEI juxtaposed to an enlargement of the 1976 Solsearch Architects sectional perspective drawing of the family greenhouse and dwelling.
7.02d Full scale mockup of the Ark kitchen greenhouse, with video screen showing Japanese NHK television film of life in the Ark.

7.02a

7.02c

7.02b

7.02d

Notes

Assessing the Ark

1 See, for example, Greg Castillo, editor, *Hippie Modernism: The Struggle for Utopia* (Minneapolis: Walker Art Center, 2015), the catalog for an exhibition of the same name, and Felicity Scott, *Outlaw Territories: Environments of Insecurity/ Architectures of Counterinsurgency* (New York: Verso, 2016).

Chapter 1 The Ark Moment: Celebrating an Ecological Dreamscape

1 Details of the Ark's principles are provided in Chapter 2. A basic description and documentation of the Ark is provided in Steven Mannell, *Atlantic Modern: The Architecture of the Atlantic Provinces, 1950-2000* (Halifax NS: TUNS Press, 2004), 60-63. Background information is provided in Alan MacEachern, *The Institute of Man and Resources: An Environmental Fable* (Charlottetown PEI: Island Studies Press, 2003), 21-25, 35-36.

2 Solsearch Architects, *The PEI Ark* poster, n.d. The poster was designed and printed in late 1976 or early 1977. Ole Hammarlund, interview by author, 26 July 2016.

3 The Ark's "ecological architecture" aligns with Sim Van der Ryn and Stuart Cowan's definition of "ecological design," which is design that "minimizes environmentally destructive impacts by integrating itself with living processes." Sim Van der Ryn and Stuart Cowan, *Ecological Design* (Washington DC: Island Press, 2010), 18. As will be argued in Chapter 4, the Ark seeks to go beyond "harm reduction" to propose a positive collaboration with nature.

4 *Journal of the New Alchemists* 1 (1973): inside front cover. This motto was printed above a description of the Institute and its goals, operations and membership options on the inside front cover of each Journal, and was also printed at the top of its letterhead.

5 E.F. Schumacher, *Small is Beautiful: Economics as if People Mattered* (New York: Harper & Row, 1973). Schumacher's ideas and influence are discussed in Chapter 2.

6 The relationship of the Ark project to Habitat '76 is discussed in Chapter 2.

7 Charlottetown *Guardian*, 21 October 1976, 35.

8 Pierre Elliott Trudeau, "From Urgencies to Essentials," *The CoEvolution Quarterly* 12 (Winter 1976/77): 102-103. According to Bruce McCallum, Trudeau's speechwriter Joy Kogawa (later a well-known novelist) was influential in building Trudeau's interest in the Ark and Appropriate Technology. She and her then-partner John Flanders, an architecture professor at Carleton University with an interest in environmental design, were both members of the "eco-network" then developing in Ottawa. Bruce McCallum, "My Involvement with the PEI Ark Project," *The PEI Ark Online Catalogue*, last modifed February 2, 2017, http://peiark.com/2017/02/my-involvement-with-the-pei-ark-project/. The phrase "living lightly on the earth" was drawn from the work of ecological poet Gary Snyder. Nancy Jack Todd, *Journal of the New Alchemists* 2 (1974): 3.

9 J. Baldwin, "The New Alchemists," *The CoEvolution Quarterly* 12 (Winter 1976/77): 108.

10 John Todd interview, in Mary O'Connell, "Was Small Beautiful?" *Ideas*, radio program (16 March 2004; Toronto: Canadian Broadcasting Corporation). Todd says Trudeau made this remark to Nancy Jack Todd during the tour. Nancy Jack Todd, *A Safe and Sustainable World: The Promise of Ecological Design* (Washington: Island Press, 2006), 111, repeats the anecdote and locates the conversation at the Ark's dining table, overlooking the kitchen greenhouse.

11 Nancy Jack Todd, "Opening the Arks," *Journal of the New Alchemists* 4 (1977): 16.

12 Nancy Willis interview, 18 September 2015. Earle Barnhart says Blackett told him that it was to preserve her hair for church the next morning, which was a more important occasion than the Prime Minister's visit (however the opening was on a Tuesday, so the party seems the more likely reason). Earle Barnhart, email to author, 19 May 2016. Blackett later worked as the Ark's cleaner.

13 Nancy Jack Todd, "Opening the Arks," 16.

14 Baldwin, "The New Alchemists," 108.

15 Nancy Jack Todd, "Opening the Arks," 15-16.

16 Stewart Brand, editor's note, *The CoEvolution Quarterly* 12 (Winter 1976/77): 103.

17 Sandra Gwyn, "The Capital: If the deluge hits, head for Spry Point, P.E.I. (Ottawa is building an Ark)," *Saturday Night*, October 1976, 11.

18 Editorial, "Urgent preparations for the future," *Globe and Mail*, 29 September 1976, 6.

19 Nancy Jack Todd, *A Safe and Sustainable World*, 113.

20 New Alchemy Institute, *An Ark for Prince Edward Island: A Report to the Federal Government of Canada* (Souris PE: New Alchemy Institute, 1976), frontispiece. Prime Minister Trudeau signed a paper version of this dedication at the opening ceremony. It was reproduced with the signature on the cover of the *Report*, and seems to have been installed in some durable form at the entrance to the Ark; if so, this version was lost. David Bergmark and Ole Hammarlund, interview by author, 17 September 2015; Willis interview, 18 September 2015.

21 Ole Hammarlund and David Bergmark, "The Architects' View," *Journal of the New Alchemists* 3 (1976): 44. The collector glass was an optical glass with smooth exterior and faceted interior faces, to increase diffusion of

sunlight. David Bergmark, email to author, 28 February 2017.

22 2x4 studs with fibreglass batts and no exterior sheathing insulation were the norm for residential and light frame construction in the 1970s. The 2x6 studs, thicker batt insulation, and exterior sheathing insulation used at the Ark became the norm for energy-efficient buildings by the mid-1980s. Ole Hammarlund, email to author, 25 July 2016.

23 David Bergmark, email to author, 03 August 2016.

24 David Bergmark, email to author, 03 August 2016. Bergmark characterized the system as a "thermal flywheel."

25 John Todd interview, "The Ark Part 1: Sun for All Seasons," *Land & Sea,* television program (1977; Charlottetown: Canadian Broadcasting Corporation).

26 R. Dalton Muir, *A Most Prudent Ark* (Ottawa: Fisheries and Environment Canada/ Ministry of Supply and Services, 1977), 9.

27 Muir, Prudent Ark, 7-9; Ron Zweig, "The Saga of the Solar-Algae Ponds," *Journal of the New Alchemists* 4 (1977): 63-68.

28 Nancy Jack Todd, "Bioshelters and Their Implications for Lifestyle," *Habitat: An International Journal* v2 n1/2 (1977): 98.

29 New Alchemy Institute PEI, *Quarterly Report September – December 1977* (Souris PE: New Alchemy Institute, 1977), 96.

30 Muir, *Prudent Ark*, 9. The use of hydraulics was unusual, and extended previous New Alchemy windmill experiments using compressed air to drive equipment. The energy required to lift hydraulic fluid to the top of the Hydrowind tower was a major unanticipated weakness of the design; the variable-pitch vanes were also a complication. Earle Barnhart, email to author, 26 July 2016.

31 Muir, *Prudent Ark*, 12.

32 Early media stories suggested that John and Nancy Jack Todd and their children would take on the "mission" to live in the Ark, or that various New Alchemist families would take it in quarterly turns. See for example Barbara McAndrew, "PEI chosen for ecological ark plan to perfect self-sufficient living unit," *Globe and Mail,* 4 July 1975, B1; "Urgent Preparations for the Future," 6. "

33 A four-minute silent film made by NHK Japanese television in February 1977 provides an overview of daily life in the Ark (Nancy Willis collection). See also "The Ark Part 1: Sun for All Seasons," and "The Ark Part 2: Within Our Limits," *Land & Sea,* television program (1977; Charlottetown: Canadian Broadcasting Corporation); Dorothy Todd Hénaut, *Sun, Wind, and Wood,* film (1977; Montreal: National Film Board of Canada); Dorothy and Bob Fletcher, "The Ark: Habitat Concept for the Future," *Canadian Geographical Journal* (June/ July 1977): 56-59; David Lees, "Aboard the Good Ship Ark," *Harrowsmith* 9, vol. 2 no. 3 (September/October 1977): 48-53, 82-83, 97-98; Constance Mungall, "Space-Age Ark: Brave New Home," *Chatelaine* v50 n11 (November 1977): 52-53, 102-104, 106, 108-109; Robert Argue, *The Sun Builders: A People's Guide to Solar, Wind and Wood Energy in Canada* (Toronto: Renewable Energy in Canada, 1978): 30-33.

34 New Alchemy Institute, *An Ark for Prince Edward Island: A Report to the Federal Government of Canada,* "Part 1: The Ark" (Souris PE: New Alchemy Institute, 1976), 71.

35 Mungall, "Space-Age Ark: Brave New Home," 109.

36 David Bergmark interview, "The Ark Part 1: Sun for All Seasons."

37 McCallum, "My Involvement with the PEI Ark."

Chapter 2 New Alchemy: Appropriate Technology for Canada's Future

1 The background and context of the Ark are covered in several recent sources, notably Alan MacEachern, *The Institute of Man and Resources: An Environmental Fable* (Charlottetown PE: Island Studies Press, 2003); Henry Trim, "Experts at Work: The Canadian State, North American Environmentalism, and Renewable Energy in an Era of Limits, 1968-1983" (PhD dissertation, University of British Columbia, 2014); Henry Trim, "An Ark for the Future: Science, Technology and the Canadian back-to-the-Land Movement of the 1970s," in Colin Coates, ed., *Canadian Countercultures and the Environment* (Calgary: University of Calgary Press, 2016), 153-177.

2 Rachel Carson, *Silent Spring* (Boston: Houghton Mifflin, 1962).

3 Jacques Grinevald, "Introduction," in Vladimr Vernadsky, *The Biosphere* (New York: Copernicus/ Springer, 1997), 22. This definition is by British plant geographer Nicholas Polunin based upon the work of Russian mineralogist Vernadsky published in 1926. The term "biosphere" was coined by the Austrian geologist Eduard Suess in 1875. The 1968 UN Conference on the Biosphere in Paris was marked by publication of a special "Biosphere" issue of *Scientific American* in September 1970, which popularized the concept.

4 Andrew Kirk, *Counterculture Green: The Whole Earth Catalog and American Environmentalism* (Lawrence: University Press of Kansas, 2011), 42-43; Christine Macy and Sarah Bonnemaison, *Architecture and Nature: Creating the American Landscape* (London: Routledge, 2003), 293. Frank White, *The Overview Effect: Space Exploration and Human Evolution* (Boston: Houghton Mifflin, 1987), tracks actual effects of space exploration and space-based imagery on astronauts and on human society; White supports Brand's thesis of a transformation of human conceptions of environment and society resulting from viewing the "whole earth" from space.

5 Paul R. Ehrlich, *The Population Bomb* (New York: Ballantine Books, 1971); Donella H. Meadows, Dennis L. Meadows, Jørgen Randers, and William W. Behrens III, *The Limits to Growth* (New York: Universe Books, 1972).

6 Strong was a former oil patch entrepreneur, and was called upon by
   Trudeau to lead Petro-Canada from 1976 to 1978.

7 Pierre Elliott Trudeau speech, in Mary O'Connell, "Was Small
   Beautiful?" *Ideas*, radio program (16 March 2004; Toronto: Canadian
   Broadcasting Corporation).

8 Trim, "Experts at Work," 141-147. These policies were in fact not new,
   but extended the pre-OPEC policy of managed prices, which until
   1973 saw eastern Canadians paying above the world price for their
   imported oil, with the tariff going to subsidize prices for western
   consumers of high-cost Alberta oil. Not surprisingly, this "balancing"
   led the western provinces to resent the rest of the country.

9 MacEachern, *The Institute of Man and Resources*, 15.

10 The Science Council seems to have been intended to fulfil a role
   analogous to that of the Canada Council for the Arts in the 1950s, to
   both bolster the science sector, and to increase its capacity to advance
   Canadian society. The discussion of the Science Council here draws
   on Trim, "Experts at Work," 113-152. See also Henry Trim, "Planning
   the Future: The Conserver Society and Canadian Sustainability," *The
   Canadian Historical Review* vol. 96 no. 3 (September 2013): 375-404.

11 Science Council of Canada, *Report No. 19: Natural Resource Policy
   Issues in Canada* (Ottawa: Information Canada, 1973), 39.

12 Robert Paehlke, "Canada: Toward a Conserver Society," *Environment*,
   vol. 20 no. 3 (April 1978): 5.

13 Science Council of Canada, *Report No. 27: Canada as a Conserver
   Society* (Ottawa: Minister of Supply and Services Canada, 1977); E.F.
   Schumacher, *Small is Beautiful: Economics as if People Mattered* (New
   York: Harper & Row, 1973); Kenneth E. Boulding, "The Economics
   of the Coming Spaceship Earth," in Henry Jerrett, ed., *Environmental
   Quality in a Growing Economy: Essays from the Sixth Resources for the
   Future Forum*, (Baltimore: Johns Hopkins University Press, 1966), 3-14.

14 Trim, "Experts at Work," 138-141. Science Council of Canada, *Report
   No. 27: Canada as a Conserver Society*, 50-55, 77-81.

15 Stewart Brand, editor's note, *The CoEvolution Quarterly* 12 (Winter
   1976/77): 102-103.

16 See Mirko Zardini, Harriet Russell, Giovanna Borasi, and Adam
   Bobbette, *Sorry, Out of Gas! Architecture's Response to the 1973 Oil
   Crisis* (Montreal: Canadian Centre for Architecture, 2007), 192-223;
   also Nishat Awan, Tatjana Schneider, and Jeremy Till, *Spatial agency:
   Other Ways of Doing Architecture* (Abingdon: Routledge, 2011)
   provides short encyclopedia-style entries on most of these groups.
   Macy and Bonnemaison, *Architecture and Nature*, 333-338, discusses
   the Farallones Institute's Integral House project.

17 Kelvin W. Willoughby, *Technology Choice: A Critique of the Appropriate
   Technology Movement* (London: Intermediate Technology

Publications, 1990): 342, 340.

18 For example, Peter Harper and Godfrey Boyle, *Radical Technology*
   (London: Undercurrents, 1976), 57.

19 The exchange of information and passions in this era had a different
   dynamic than today's instant download gratification: A slow process
   of anticipation would start by reviewing a list of titles and summaries,
   making selections, filling out an order form, buying a money order
   from the bank (or sending cash), and waiting for a big envelope in the
   mail. One can imagine all the little envelopes of order forms making
   their way around the planet, resulting in chubby big brown envelopes
   of liberating information and plans.

20 New Alchemy Institute, *An Ark for Prince Edward Island: A Family Sized
   Food, Energy, and Housing Complex, Including Integrated Solar,
   Windmill, Greenhouse, Fish Culture, and Living Components* (Woods
   Hole MA: New Alchemy Institute, 1975): 44 (New Alchemy Vertical
   File, University of Prince Edward Island Special Collections).

21 Stewart Brand, *Whole Earth Catalog: Access to Tools* (Menlo Park
   CA: Portola Institute, 1969). Brand attended the opening of the PEI
   Ark in 1976. In contrast to Prime Minister Trudeau's helicopters,
   Brand borrowed the "Evening Star," an eighteen-foot, gaff-rigged,
   traditionally built open wooden boat and sailed over to Spry Point
   from Cape Breton Island. He reported barely surviving the trip, which
   took almost three days. This voyage offers an iconic (if extreme)
   example of what Alternative Technology means – more directly
   engaging, more effortful, but perhaps also more meaningful. AT
   implies considerations of the meaning and implications of the use
   of a technology, beyond simply assessing the effective outcome of
   the technology. Trudeau's use of an entourage of two helicopters to
   attend the opening of the Ark has, to our eyes, a remarkable load of
   ironic and contradictory implications. For a photo of the boat and
   descriptive caption see *The CoEvolution Quarterly* 12: 111.

22 Alastair Gordon, *Spaced Out: Radical Environments of the Psychedelic
   Sixties* (New York: Rizzoli, 2008). Gordon's "Part II: Outlaw Nation"
   offers a rich presentation and analysis of these explorations.

23 Gordon, *Spaced Out*, 103, 145. Gordon denotes McLuhan's ideas about
   the pending disintegration of cities and a return to tribal clusters as a
   "retribalization," and links this concept to Buckminster Fuller's call for
   the ephemeralization of the built environment. Marshall McLuhan,
   Understanding Media (London: Routledge & Kegan Paul, 1964),
   4-5; R. Buckminster Fuller, *Operating Manual for Spaceship Earth*
   (Carbondale: Southern Illinois University Press, 1969); R. Buckminster
   Fuller, Joachim Krausse, and Claude Lichtenstein, *Your Private Sky: R.
   Buckminster Fuller: Art Design Science* (Baden: Lars Müller Publishers,
   1999), 457. Macy and Bonnemaison, *Architecture and Nature*, 323-

333 considers the interaction of Fuller's work and the counterculture.

24 *The Digger Papers*, August 1968, http://www.diggers.org/diggers/digger_papers_1968.pdf; quoted in Gordon, *Spaced Out*, 127.

25 Brand, editor's note, *The CoEvolution Quarterly* 12, 103.

26 Ursula Franklin, *The Ursula Franklin Reader: Pacifism as a Map* (Toronto: Between the Lines, 2006), 137; Ursula Franklin, *The Real World of Technology* (Toronto: CBC Enterprises, 1990), 12.

27 Nancy Jack Todd, *A Safe and Sustainable World: The Promise of Ecological Design* (Washington: Island Press, 2006), 6; Susan Soucoup, "Prince Edward's Ark: Bringing the Homestead Indoors on Prince Edward Island," *Harrowsmith 2*, vol. 1 no. 2 (July/ August 1976): 33.

28 Nancy Jack Todd and John Todd, *From Eco-cities to Living Machines: Principles of Ecological Design* (Berkeley CA: North Atlantic Books, 1996), 3.

29 Nicholas Wade, "New Alchemy Institute: Search for an Alternative Agriculture," *Science* 187 (4178) (28 February 1975): 727, 729.

30 John Todd, "The New Alchemists," *The CoEvolution Quarterly* 9 (Spring 1976): 55.

31 John Todd, "Tomorrow is Our Permanent Address," *Journal of the New Alchemists* 4 (1977): 89.

32 The New Alchemy farm was the site of the working research community; the New Alchemists lived independently in Woods Hole and other neighbouring communities.

33 Todd, "The New Alchemists," *CoEvolution Quarterly* 9, 62-63.

34 John Todd interview, "The Ark Part 2: Within Our Limits," *Land & Sea*, television program (1977; Charlottetown: Canadian Broadcasting Corporation).

35 Wade, "New Alchemy," 729. After the Arks were built, New Alchemy did receive one significant grant from the US National Science Foundation for a program of monitoring and modelling the performance of the Cape Cod Ark. See Nancy Jack Todd, "New Alchemy: Creation Myth and Ongoing Saga," *Journal of the New Alchemists* 6 (1981): 14.

36 Nancy Jack Todd, ed., *The Book of the New Alchemists* (New York: Dutton, 1977). For a sketch of the history and production process of the Journal, see Nancy Jack Todd, "Overview," *Journal of the New Alchemists* 5 (1979): 7-8.

37 Stewart Brand, editor's note, *The CoEvolution Quarterly* 9 (Spring 1976): 55.

38 Paul Van Slambrouk, "Life in a Self - Sufficient Greenhouse," *Christian Science Monitor* (22 November 1978): 1.

39 Dorothy Todd Hénaut, *The New Alchemists,* film (1974; Montreal: National Film Board of Canada). Hénaut was John Todd's sister.

40 Hénaut, *The New Alchemists,* shows Hess assisting with cleaning and cooking before declaring his satisfaction with the fish.

41 David Bergmark, email to author, 03 August 2016.

42 David Bergmark interview, in O'Connell, "Was Small Beautiful?"

43 Robert Angevine, Earle Barnhart and John Todd, "New Alchemy's Ark: A Proposed Solar Heat and Wind Powered Greenhouse and Aquaculture Complex Adapted to Northern Climates," *Journal of the New Alchemists* 2 (1974): 35-43.

44 John Todd interview, in O'Connell, "Was Small Beautiful?"

45 James K. Page Jr and Wilson Clark, "The New Alchemy: How to Survive in Your Spare Time," *Smithsonian* vol. 5 no. 11 (February 1975): 82-89; Barry Conn Hughes, "The World That Feeds Itself," *The Canadian Magazine* (9 February 1974): 2-4, 7.

46 John Todd, letter to Andrew Wells and David Catmur, 29 January 1975; accompanied by John Todd, "Weathering Collapsing Global Economic Systems: A Blueprint for Prince Edward Island," 29 January 1975 (Series 5, General Files, 1974-83, subseries 2, Ark Reports, IMR Fonds, Provincial Archives of Prince Edward Island).

47 John Todd and Nancy Jack Todd, "Land and Its Use: Costa Rica" *Journal of the New Alchemists* 1 (1973): 12-46.

48 Nancy Jack Todd, *A Safe and Sustainable World*, 98.

49 Hughes, "The World That Feeds Itself," 4. It is unclear what first drew Todd to suggest PEI; perhaps the sense that Campbell's government was sympathetic. The Ark's concept resonated with the motivations of back-to-the-land youth communes, which were a response to contemporary anxieties—especially felt in urban areas in the USA of the 1970s—about the sustainability of urban life. PEI welcomed a large number of self-styled urban refugees in the 1970s; these "Back to the (Is)landers" were motivated by a romance of a return to a simpler, more direct, self-sufficient and do-it-yourself rural lifestyle, but also by the perception that PEI would be clear of the likely radiation fallout pathways in the event of a Soviet nuclear attack on the USA. For more on the PEI counterculture, see Alan MacEachern and Ryan O'Connor, *Back to the Island: The Back-to-the-Land Movement on PEI*, last modified 2009, http://niche-canada.org/member-projects/backtotheisland/home.html.

50 New Alchemy Institute, *An Ark for Prince Edward Island* (1975): 10. The same passage reports that the article received more reader responses than any previous article in the magazine's history.

51 Bruce McCallum, Advanced Concepts Centre, *Environmentally Appropriate Technology: Renewable Energy and Other Developing Technologies for a Conserver Society in Canada* (Ottawa: Fisheries and Environment Canada, 1975).

52 See Chapter 1, note 7.

53 Bruce McCallum, "My Involvement with the PEI Ark Project," *The PEI*

Ark Online Catalogue, last modified February 2, 2017, http://peiark.com/2017/02/my-involvement-with-the-pei-ark-project/.

54 John Todd, letter to Bruce McCallum, 4 August 1974 (Bruce McCallum papers); McCallum, "My Involvement with the PEI Ark."

55 H. Wade MacLauchlan, *Alex B. Campbell: The Prince Edward Island Premier Who Rocked the Cradle* (Charlottetown: Prince Edward Island Museum and Heritage Foundation, 2014), 242.

56 MacEachern, *The Institute of Man and Resources*, 17.

57 MacEachern, *The Institute of Man and Resources*, 14.

58 MacLauchlan, *Alex B. Campbell,* 258-260.

59 MacEachern, *The Institute of Man and Resources*, 20-22.

60 Robert W. Durie, letter to John Todd, 28 October 1974 (Series 5, General Files 8, 1974-83, subseries 2, The Ark Project, IMR Fonds, Provincial Archives of Prince Edward Island).

61 Bruce McCallum notes that Wells had met Douglas at the 1974 UN World Population Conference in Bucharest; they later married and Douglas moved to PEI in 1975. McCallum, "My Involvement with the PEI Ark."

62 Urban Affairs Canada, *The Canadian Urban Demonstration Program* (Ottawa: Ministry of State for Urban Affairs, 1975), 7-11. The CUDP emphasized "demonstration projects" rather than ideas or concepts. Primary selection criteria sought projects with Canada-wide significance; that were solution-oriented; departed from conventional practices; and that accounted for interactions with the environment. Secondary criteria included use of local skills and resources, and reducing social inequality. Guidelines showed the CUDP expected a public demonstration and a formal evaluation of effectiveness.

63 Lynne Douglas, email to author, 26 February 2017.

64 John Todd, email to author, 20 March 2017.

65 Russell J. Irvine, letter to John Todd, 14 January 1975; Todd, letter to Irvine, 10 February 1975 (Earle Barnhart papers).

66 New Alchemy Institute, *An Ark for Prince Edward Island* (1975).

67 Earle Barnhart and Hilde Maingay, interview by author, 14 May 2015.

68 Earle Barnhart, "Design Principles" handwritten notes, n.d. [likely October-November 1974], (Earle Barnhart papers). Barnhart's sources cited in these notes include Victor Olgyay, *Design with Climate* (Princeton NJ: Princeton University Press, 1973); Bruce N. Anderson, *Solar Energy and Shelter Design* (Harrisville: Anderson, 1973); J. Maghsood, "A study of solar energy parameters in plastic-covered greenhouses" *Journal of Agricultural Engineering Research* 21 (3) (1976): 305-312 (presumably a pre-publication draft); and Elvin McDonald, *Handbook for Greenhouse Gardeners* (Irvington-on-Hudson, NY: Lord & Burnham, 1972).

69 Ministry of State for Urban Affairs Press Release, "First Urban Demonstration Projects Receive Federal Approval," 15 April 1975

70 Chris Dennett, "Ecological 'ark' in P.E.I. to run on wind and sun," *Toronto Star*, 12 April 1976, B3.

71 MacEachern, *The Institute of Man and Resources*, 29; MacLauchlan, *Alex B. Campbell,* 265-266.

72 MacLauchlan, *Alex B. Campbell,* 264.

73 MacEachern, *The Institute of Man and Resources*, 20.

74 MacEachern, *The Institute of Man and Resources*, 21.

75 MacEachern, *The Institute of Man and Resources*, 33. IMR's initiatives were diverse: it was involved in establishing the Atlantic Wind Test site at North Cape, PE in 1978, and in building a combined heat and power plant fuelled by solid waste and serving a district heating network for the entire city of Charlottetown. It commissioned highly-insulated, energy efficient housing plans that were precursors to the later R-2000 homes standard, and fostered the development of high-efficiency wood pellet stoves and boilers. It produced newsletters, guides, tips and fact sheets to help Islanders make better choices about energy and systems, backed up by direct technical support.

76 MacEachern, *The Institute of Man and Resources*, 28-31. Energy Days was televised live on CBC and covered widely in the international alternative technology press.

77 John Todd, "The Ark Part 2: Within Our Limits."

(Acc 91-009 "Ark (c) Reports, Results 2000-7, 1978-81, Series 5.2 General Files, IMR Fonds, PEI Archives).

Chapter 3 Solsearch Architects: Designing an Ecological Architecture

1 Barbara McAndrew, "PEI chosen for ecological ark plan to perfect self-sufficient living unit," *Globe and Mail*, 4 July 1975, B1; Ministry of State for Urban Affairs Press Release, "First Urban Demonstration Projects Receive Federal Approval," 15 April 1975 (Acc 91-009 "Ark (c) Reports, Results 2000-7, 1978-81, Series 5.2 General Files, IMR Fonds, PEI Archives). Although the decisions about winning projects were made as early as January 1975 (based on communications with the New Alchemists) the public announcement was delayed until mid-April. The CUDP was cancelled by the Minister a few months later, in July.

2 David Bergmark and Ole Hammarlund, interview by author, 10-11 December 2015.

3 Bergmark and Hammarlund interview, 10-11 December 2015.

4 Nancy Willis, interview by author, 18 September 2015.

5 Earle Barnhart and Hilde Maingay, interview by author, 14 May 2015.

6 Bernard Flaman, *Architecture of Saskatchewan: A Visual Journey*, 1930-2011 (Regina: Canadian Plains Research Centre Press, 2013), 108-109.

7 Ole Hammarlund, email to author, 25 July 2016

8 Bergmark and Hammarlund interview, 10-11 December 2015.

9 Bergmark and Hammarlund interview, 10-11 December 2015.

10 Nancy Jack Todd, "Opening the Arks," *Journal of the New Alchemists* 4 (1977): 12.

11 Ole Hammarlund and David Bergmark, "The Architects' View," *Journal of the New Alchemists* 3 (1976): 44.

12 Hammarlund and Bergmark, "The Architects' View," 44.

13 Bergmark and Hammarlund interview, 10-11 December 2015.

14 See Chapter 1, note 33.

15 John Todd, "An Ark for Prince Edward Island," *Journal of the New Alchemists* 3 (1976): 42.

16 David Bergmark and Ole Hammarlund, interview by author, 17 September 2015; Laura Engstrom, "The Six-Pack: A Backyard Solar Greenhouse," *Journal of the New Alchemists* 4 (1977): 124. Detailed drawings of the Six-Pack were published with the Engstrom article; these drawings were made after construction was complete.

17 Nancy Jack Todd, "New Alchemy: Creation Myth and Ongoing Saga," *Journal of the New Alchemists* 6 (1980): 13.

18 Engstrom, "The Six-Pack," 125, notes that the Six-Pack's basic configuration was based on a northern-climate solar greenhouse designed by the Brace Research Institute of McGill University's McDonald Agricultural College, which pioneered the asymmetrical arrangement of glazed south slope and solid insulated north slope to reduce heat loss, with a reflective surface on the interior of the north slope to compensate for the reduced glazing. The Brace design was studied by Earle Barnhart in preparation for the original Habitat '76 version of the Ark design, but in Barnhart's Ark design the important reflective north interior wall was occupied instead by solar panels. J. Maghsood, "A study of solar energy parameters in plastic-covered greenhouses" *Journal of Agricultural Engineering Research*, vol. 21, no. 3 (1976): 305-312. Also T.A. Lawand, R. Alward, B. Saulnier, and E. Brunet, "The development and testing of an environmentally designed greenhouse for colder regions," *Solar Energy, vol.* 17, no. 5 (11, 1975): 307; and T.A. Lawand, R. Alward, B. Saulnier, and E. Brunet, *Solar Energy Greenhouses: Operating Experiences* (Montreal: Brace Research Institute, Macdonald College of McGill University, 1976).

19 David Bergmark, email to author, 03 August 2016.

20 Barnhart and Maingay interview, 14 May 2015.

21 Bergmark email, 03 August 2016.

22 The Suntube tanks were promoted in the Journal, and Kalwall started a special division to manufacture the tanks for aquaculture in a variety of sizes, which is still in operation in 2017. Todd noted that use of the tanks had spread to dozens of aquaculture operations within 18 months. John Todd interview, "The Ark Part 2: Within Our Limits," *Land & Sea*, television program (1977; Charlottetown: Canadian Broadcasting Corporation).

23 John Todd interview, "The Ark Part 1: Sun for All Seasons," *Land & Sea*, television program (1977; Charlottetown: Canadian Broadcasting Corporation).

24 Engstrom, "The Six-Pack," 126.

25 Sean Wellesley-Miller and Day Chahroudi, with Marguerite Villecco, "Bioshelter," *Architecture Plus* (November-December 1974): 90-95. The reprint copy with John Todd's note is among Earle Barnhart's papers.

26 Wellesley-Miller and Chahroudi, "Bioshelter," 91.

27 Wellesley-Miller and Chahroudi, "Bioshelter," 91. The article describes proposed developments of Suntek that would maintain a thin layer of thermostatic "cloud gel" to provide integral temperature-responsive sun shading and insulation, with the possibility of chemical or biological energy conversion within the film layers.

28 Wellesley-Miller and Chahroudi, "Bioshelter," 91.

29 Bergmark and Hammarlund interview, 17 September 2015; New Alchemy Institute, *An Ark for Prince Edward Island: A Report to the Federal Government of Canada,* "Part 1: The Ark," (Souris, PE: New Alchemy Institute, 1976), 20, 39.

30 Bergmark and Hammarlund interview, 17 September 2015.

31 Bergmark email, 03 August 2016.

32 Ole Hammarlund, email to author, 26 July 2016. This growing design commitment to the greenhouse as architecture had a contemporary parallel in John Hix's *The Glass House* (Cambridge MA: MIT Press, 1974) which presented the history of the greenhouse as the first "conditioned" environment, in which meeting the needs of the inhabitants (here exotic plants and fauna) was a paramount factor in form and design, and environmental systems were fully integrated with the fabric (rather than being tacked-on equipment such as fireplaces, plumbing, electrical systems, or even insulation layers). The first edition concluded with chapters presenting speculative designs using the greenhouse as a basis for enhanced human architecture, including Brenda Vale's first student design for an "Autonomous House" using the greenhouse in a manner similar to the PEI Ark, for both food production and environmental buffering. Solsearch used illustrations from Hix's book as historical precedents in post-Ark presentations of their greenhouse-integrated designs (Solsearch slide files, Bergmark Guimond Hammarlund Jones Architects, Charlottetown, PE). Hix was the designer of Provident House in Aurora, ON (1976), a single family house with solar heating, water storage, and a small integrated greenhouse; it was also selected for

funding under the Urban Demonstration Program. John Hix, "3 Solar Energy Projects: Provident House," *Canadian Architect*, vol. 22, no. 3, (March 1977): 34-35.

33 According to David Bergmark, the Rohaglas acrylic sheet was preferred to standard (and more durable) polycarbonate greenhouse glazing because it transmitted ultra-violet light, and the wider light spectrum was thought to provide for better plant growth. Bergmark email, 03 August 2016. Earle Barnhart notes that it was later determined that the ultraviolet light was not significant for photosynthesis, only visible light. Earle Barnhart, email to author, 11 September 2016.

34 Bergmark email, 03 August 2016.

35 Hammarlund and Bergmark, "The Architects' View," 44.

36 Todd, "An Ark for Prince Edward Island," 42.

37 Todd, "An Ark for Prince Edward Island," 41.

38 "Cancellation of UDP," *Ottawa Journal*, 04 July 1975, 10. Telegram from Minister: New Alchemy Institute, *An Ark for Prince Edward Island: A Report*, "Part 1: The Ark," 19.

39 Bergmark and Hammarlund interview, 10-11 December 2015.

40 Bruce McCallum, "My Involvement with the PEI Ark Project," *The PEI Ark Online Catalogue*, last modifed February 2, 2017, http://peiark.com/2017/02/my-involvement-with-the-pei-ark-project/.

41 Barnhart and Maingay interview, 14 May 2015; Bergmark and Hammarlund interview, 10-11 December 2015.

42 Bergmark and Hammarlund interview, 10-11 December 2015.

43 Ole Hammarlund, email to author, 24 February 2017.

44 A 1975 Popular Science article on solar energy for houses featured examples by Sunworks, including an installation in a house designed by architect Charles W. Moore, Barber's colleague at Yale. Richard Stepler, "Now You Can Buy Solar Heating Equipment For Your Home," *Popular Science* (March 1975): 76-77.

45 As-built drawings showing the actual construction and details of the Ark were made in the fall of 1976, but dated October 1975, as discussed in Chapter 4.

46 Compared to the standard polycarbonate version, the acrylic Rohaglas had 10 percent better light transmission, which was significant for photosynthesis and heat gains. Hammarlund email, 24 February 2017; David Bergmark, email to author, 06 March 2017.

47 According to David Bergmark "by this time we had calculated light transmission for many different glazing systems and by this point we were very sensitive that adding layers of glazing or shutters had a significant impact on reducing light penetration and therefore impacted energy and plant production." Bergmark email, 03 August 2016.

48 Hammarlund email, 25 July 2016.

49 John Todd, letter to Robert Durie, 11 September 1975 (Earle Barnhart Papers); New Alchemy Institute, *An Ark for Prince Edward Island: A Report*, "Part 1: The Ark," 20.

50 Bergmark email, 03 August 2016.

51 The quest for rock was long and difficult; the project timeline notes that in May 1976 they "finally located source of rocks in Nova Scotia for the hot air-rock storage system." New Alchemy Institute, *An Ark for Prince Edward Island: A Report*, "Part 1: The Ark," 21.

52 Earl Davison of Provincial Boat and Marine in Kensington, PE; David Bergmark, email to author 27 February 2017; Ole Hammarlund, email to author, 27 February 2017.

53 Nancy Willis, interview by author, 18 September 2015.

54 Chris Dennett, "Ecological 'ark' in P.E.I. to run on wind and sun," Toronto *Star*, 12 April 1976, B3. Ole Hammarlund remarked that with just a temporary enclosure of polyethylene sheeting, the passive solar performance of the greenhouse was sufficient to create a pleasant working environment for winter construction. Hammarlund email, 26 July 2016.

55 Bergmark and Hammarlund interview, 03 November 2014; Hammarlund email, 25 July 2016.

56 Willis interview, 18 September 2015.

57 Nancy Jack Todd, "Opening the Arks," 14.

58 J. Baldwin, "The New Alchemists," *The CoEvolution Quarterly* 12 (Winter 1976/77): 106.

59 Baldwin, "The New Alchemists," 106. Baldwin reported that according to the grader driver, this pond "just happened to be official hockey rink size."

60 Baldwin, "The New Alchemists," 108. According to Earle Barnhart, Bob Angevine, who had served in Vietnam, was seen to cock his head and call "choppers" several minutes before anyone else saw or heard them. Earle Barnhart, email to author, 19 May 2016.

Chapter 4 The Ark's Life and Legacy

1 Ole Hammarlund, email to author, 25 July 2016. Keptin John Joe Sark confirmed that he officiated at the Ark ceremony, Lynne Douglas, email to author, 27 February 2017.

2 Nancy Jack Todd, "Opening the Arks," *Journal of the New Alchemists* 4 (1977): 16. Nancy Willis, David Bergmark and Ole Hammarlund were too exhausted by the rush of final preparations to attend either ceremony. Hammarlund email, 25 July 2016; Nancy Willis, email message to author, 20 February 2017.

3 New Alchemy Institute PEI, *Quarterly Report September – December 1977* (Souris, PE: New Alchemy Institute, 1977), 101.

4 Ian McKay, *The Quest of The Folk: Antimodernism and Cultural Selection in Twentieth-Century Nova Scotia*, (Montreal: McGill-Queen's

University Press, 2009), xv. This analysis also draws on McKay's observations about the late modern reverence for "old and traditional ways" as a source of authenticity in the face of ambivalence about progress and industrialization (178). These ideas are explored further in two previous articles by the author examining the Ark and Atlantic Canadian modern architecture in a context of antimodernity: Steven Mannell, "Modern Heritage and Folk Culture in Atlantic Canada," *Journal / International Working-Party for Documentation and Conservation of Buildings, Sites and Neighbourhoods of the Modern Movement (Docomomo)* 38 (March 2008): 83-88; Steven Mannell, "The Dream (and Lie) of Progress: Modern Heritage, Regionalism, and Folk Traditions in Atlantic Canada," *Journal of the Society for the Study of Architecture in Canada* v36 n1 (2011): 93-105.

5 John Todd, "Tomorrow is Our Permanent Address," *Journal of the New Alchemists* 4 (1977): 101.

6 Nancy Jack Todd, "Bioshelters and Their Implications for Lifestyle," *Habitat: An International Journal* v2 n1/2 (1977): 97-98.

7 Constance Mungall, "Space-Age Ark: Brave New Home," *Chatelaine* v50 n11 (November 1977): 108.

8 John Todd, "Spry Point – H. Webster Interpretation – Education Centre; New Alchemy Institute Aspects; Rural Futures – A Model," typescript proposal on New Alchemy Institute (P.E.I.) letterhead, 23 August 1976 (Earle Barnhart papers).

9 David Lees, "Aboard the Good Ship Ark," *Harrowsmith* 9, v2 n 3 ((September/ October 1977): 48-52, records the frictions of all-hours visitors and the negative perceptions of the appliances.

10 Professional design publications showed little interest in the Ark. *Canadian Architect* magazine included two pages on the Ark in a special issue on "Energy and Buildings" guest-edited by John Hix; the coverage ignored the Ark's food production systems as a component of the energy systems, and failed to credit the architects. [New Alchemy Institute], "2 The Ark for Prince Edward Island," *Canadian Architect*, v22 n3, (March 1977): 32-33. The Ark was included (and the designers credited) in a special issue of the Swiss architecture journal *Bauen + Wohnen* on "Energy and Microclimate: Points of Departure for a New Architecture" guest edited by architect Ueli Schäfer, which presented 22 examples of solar residential buildings in Canada, the USA, and western Europe. New Alchemy Institute & Solsearch Architects, "Ark on Prince Edward Island," *Bauen + Wohnen* v31 n7/8 (1977): 261-262. Articles in professional journals limited discussion to technical issues of systems and performance, while popular media such as *Chatelaine* provided a much fuller picture of the Ark vision, including an appreciation of the spatial qualities that the architecture journals ignored.

11 New Alchemy Institute, *An Ark for Prince Edward Island: A Report to the Federal Government of Canada* (Souris, PE: New Alchemy Institute, 1976), "Part 1: The Ark," 40-64. The as-built drawings are dated "October 1975" but both Bergmark and Hammarlund insist that they were not made until fall of 1976, and that the construction was guided by the August 1975 drawing set. Whether the October 1975 date was a slip of the pen (repeated on more than 20 sheets) or an effort to give the impression that the design was complete and resolved before construction started is not clear. In any case, the incorrect date obscures the reality of the on-the-fly design-build process. David Bergmark and Ole Hammarlund, interview by author, 19 July 2016.

12 New Alchemy Institute, *An Ark for Prince Edward Island: A Report,* "Part 1: The Ark," 6. The graph of "Climate vs. Ark Greenhouse Zone Performance" on p. 69 is vivid evidence of the effectiveness of the passive systems.

13 New Alchemy Institute, *An Ark for Prince Edward Island: A Report,* "Part 1: The Ark," 70. Ole Hammarlund commented "I never realized until reading your writing, but of course the heat contribution through the floor was significant, even if insulated. After all, modern radiant floors work at a very low temperature like 22 deg Celsius, and the wood floors above the tanks were bound to be at or above that temperature, even though cold to the touch." Hammarlund email, 25 July 2016.

14 New Alchemy Institute, *An Ark for Prince Edward Island: A Report,* "Part 1: The Ark," 5; Todd, "Tomorrow is Our Permanent Address," 93. Harvest statistics taken from John Todd interview, "The Ark Part 1: Sun for All Seasons," *Land & Sea,* television program (1977; Charlottetown: Canadian Broadcasting Corporation).

15 This cost includes $130,000 direct construction costs and $43,000 construction management fees; the total thus reflects what would be considered "construction costs" in budget and contract terms. Of the total $354,000 project budget, $77,000 was for design and construction of the Hydrowind; the balance of $104,000 covered architects' and other design fees, travel, and first year operations including staff salaries. Alan MacEachern comments that the New Alchemists were being disingenuous in excluding the Hydrowind and the New Alchemy soft costs from their accounts of the actual cost of the Ark. Alan MacEachern, *The Institute of Man and Resources: An Environmental Fable* (Charlottetown PE: Island Studies Press, 2003), Note 31, 129. Although these excluded costs may have been "dollars spent building the Ark," they are *not* included in conventional building industry understandings of "construction costs." In order to compare the construction cost of the Ark to conventional buildings of the day, $173,000 is the correct number.

16 Cost translations to July 2016 dollars were made using RSMeans "Historical Cost Indexes," https://www.rsmeansonline.com/references/unit/refpdf/hci.pdf

17 Ole Hammarlund interview, "The Ark Part 2: Within Our Limits," *Land & Sea*, television program (1977; Charlottetown: Canadian Broadcasting Corporation).

18 New Alchemy Institute PEI, "The New Alchemists" Ark pamphlet (Souris, PE: New Alchemy Institute PEI: [1977]).

19 New Alchemy Institute PEI, *Quarterly Report*, 25.

20 Design changes considered include raising the rear fish ponds for better solar access, inducing convection in the free greenhouse air to eliminate the ducts, and reducing night-time heat losses that had resulted when the insulated shutter system was eliminated to cut costs. As a replacement for these shutters, a simple system of insulated curtains on sliding tracks was proposed, along with an added layer of Teflon membrane at the bottom of the 2x12 joists; the shutters would have also reduced daytime overheating of the greenhouse and kitchen. David Bergmark felt that the Teflon would have reduced light transmission to an unacceptable degree. David Bergmark, email to author, 03 August 2016.

21 New Alchemy Institute PEI, *Quarterly Report*, 40.

22 New Alchemy Institute PEI, *Quarterly Report*, 42. In later years, the specialist tank environments developed for filtering aquaculture water were reimagined by the Todds as a staged sequence of filtering ecologies that became their "solar aquatic" treatment system, capable of purifying human sewage to drinking water standards. This "living machine" has been used in a number of communities around the world. See Nancy Jack Todd, *A Safe and Sustainable World: The Promise of Ecological Design* (Washington: Island Press, 2006), 154-159, 167-168.

23 New Alchemy Institute PEI, *Quarterly Report*, 66.

24 The Ark's brown trout experiment also offered an important re-stocking service to the Island when disease wiped out the trout at the Cardigan hatchery in 1977. New Alchemy Institute PEI, *Quarterly Report*, 67.

25 New Alchemy Institute PEI, *Quarterly Report*, 92.

26 Amory Lovins, "Scale, Centralization and Electrification in Energy Systems," in Irene Kiefer, ed, *Future Strategies for Energy Development: A Question of Scale, Proceedings of a Conference at Oak Ridge, Tennessee, October 20 and 21, 1976* (Oak Ridge TN: Oak Ridge Associated Universities, 1976), quoted in Todd, "Tomorrow is Our Permanent Address," 90.

27 Nancy Willis, interview by author, 18 September 2015; Mungall, "Space-Age Ark: Brave New Home," 104.

28 New Alchemy Institute PEI, *Quarterly Report*, 98.

29 Solsearch Architecture, "The Evolution of Bioshelter: Illustrated Essay," in John Todd and Nancy Jack Todd, eds, *The Village as Solar Ecology: Proceedings of The New Alchemy/ Threshold Generic Design Conference* (East Falmouth, MA: New Alchemy Institute, 1980), 48.

30 The consultant engineers were Merrill Hall and Vince Dempsey; other New Alchemists on the team were Joe Seale and Bob Angevine. New Alchemy Institute, *An Ark for Prince Edward Island: A Report*, "Part 2: Hydrowind," 1.

31 New Alchemy Institute, *An Ark for Prince Edward Island: A Family Sized Food, Energy, and Housing Complex, Including Integrated Solar, Windmill, Greenhouse, Fish Culture, and Living Components* (Woods Hole, MA: New Alchemy Institute, 1975), 3-4, 24, 26; (New Alchemy Vertical File, University of Prince Edward Island Special Collections).

32 Kelvin W. Willoughby, *Technology Choice: A Critique of the Appropriate Technology Movement* (London: Intermediate Technology Publications, 1990): 342. Willoughby points out that the decoupling of a specific instance of a technology (such as Hydrowind here) from the general mode of technology-practice envisioned by Appropriate Technology can lead to its being coopted by global consumerism. Similarly, the flexible and decentralized modes of production, intended by AT to allow for localized and participatory engagement by workers, has been adopted by neoliberal corporations to enable low-cost, globalized production. Willoughby, 333.

33 Simon Guy and Graham Farmer. "Reinterpreting Sustainable Architecture: The Place of Technology." *Journal of Architectural Education* 54, no. 3 (2001): 141-142; "Table 1," 141.

34 Guy and Farmer, 145-146; "Table 1," 141.

35 Many of those interviewed by the author and others involved with the Ark mentioned the undeserved damage to the Ark's reputation resulting from the Hydrowind cost and performance. David Bergmark and Ole Hammarlund, interview by author, 17 September 2015; Willis interview, 18 September 2015; Earle Barnhart and Hilde Maingay, interview by author, 14 May 2015; Bruce McCallum, "My Involvement with the PEI Ark Project," *The PEI Ark Online Catalogue*, last modified 02 February 2017, http://peiark.com/2017/02/my-involvement-with-the-pei-ark-project/.

36 Designed in collaboration with landscape architect (and Hammarlund's spouse) Karen Lips, and under ongoing construction in 2017. Ole Hammarlund, email to author, 16 March 2017.

37 For these projects see Solsearch Project Files, BGHJ Architects.

38 Good thermal performance resulted from R12 wall and R20 roof insulation, lapped and sealed polyethylene air barrier, 2x6 stud walls on 24 inch centres, the use of "Arkansas Framing" (a precursor to today's "Advanced Framing") to minimize thermal bridges, exterior sheathing

insulation, and pioneering pressure-treated wood foundations. "A Case Study of Heat-Retentive Homes (I) – The Solsearch 'Conserver Home.' Prince Edward Island, Canada," in Chapter 3 "Resource-Efficient Residential Architecture," U.S. Congress Office of Technology Assessment, *An Assessment of Technology for Local Development* (Washington: United States Government Printing Office, 1981), 43-45. Ole Hammarlund, email to author, 27 February 2017.

39 Hillsborough was a low-energy neighbourhood demonstration project sponsored by the Canada Mortgage and Housing Corporation, which provided a $35,000 mortgage per house ($27,000 for construction and $8,000 for land purchase). David Bergmark, interview by author, 07 March 2017; MacEachern, *The Institute of Man and Resources*, 47; "Model Houses Make Province Byword for Heating Expertise," *Globe and Mail,* 14 August 1978, 23. Media coverage of Hillsborough was positive both nationally and on the Island; even the normally hostile *Eastern Graphic* praised the Conserver One House, though pointing out that it was "a long way from the $130,000 Ark." Wally Smith, "Builds New Super Energy Efficient House: Sells for $35,000," *Eastern Graphic,* 26 April 1978.

40 The house sold for $30,000 CDN ($98,900 in 2016 dollars), and construction costs were $17 per square foot ($56 per square foot in 2016 dollars, which is very inexpensive. US housing costs at the time were $30-50/ sq ft.). 1980 costs and comparison from "A Case Study of Heat-Retentive Homes (I)," 45, 54. Cost translations to July 2016 dollars made using RSMeans "Historical Cost Indexes."

41 Ole Hammarlund, email to author, 27 July 2016.

42 Solsearch Architecture, "The Evolution of Bioshelter," 49.

43 Copernicus Watt, "Energy Savings with Passive Solar Design," *House Beautiful's Building Manual* (Fall/ Winter 1980): 115. A second Ark Two was built in Washington, CT in 1978.

44 George McRobie, *Small is Possible* (London: Abacus, 1982), 174.

45 David Miller, "Beached! An Ark Hits Sinking Sand," Toronto *Sunday Star* (2 August 1981): A14. The subtitle to a 1986 article on the renewal of the Ark is indicative: "The good news – This time it's local people doing it." Susan Mahoney, "The Resurrection of the Ark," *Atlantic Insight* (February 1987): 10. Ken Lyall, "The Ark a Waste?" in "Energy Conservation No. 1 Insert," Charlottetown *Guardian*, 29 August 1978, 3, digs quite diligently for local criticisms of the Ark and the New Alchemists. Such portrayals of local hostility to the "come-from-away" folk is not reflected by the New Alchemists; they overwhelmingly perceived the locals as welcoming and supportive, at the time and in hindsight.

46 MacEachern, *The Institute of Man and Resources*, 51-54; Henry Trim, "An Ark for the Future: Science, Technology and the Canadian back-to-the-Land Movement of the 1970s," in Colin Coates, ed., *Canadian Countercultures and the Environment* (Calgary: University of Calgary Press, 2016): 167-168. An evaluation of media coverage was part of Environment Canada's 1978 program evaluation of the Ark (which included the technical review discussed below). See J.F. Cameron, "Report on Media Coverage of the Ark, 19 January 1979" (New Alchemy Vertical File, University of Prince Edward Island Special Collections).

47 MacEachern, *The Institute of Man and Resources*, 39-48, 71-77, 83-87.

48 MacEachern, *The Institute of Man and Resources*, 29-31.

49 McCallum, "My Involvement with the PEI Ark;" E.F. Root, Chairman of the Advisory Committee on the Ark for P.E.I., memorandum to Members of the Advisory Committee (16 September 1976): 1 (Acc91-009, Background (Phasing out of Ark) 7.1, 1974-1981, Series 5.2 General Files, IMR Fonds, PEI Archives).

50 McCallum, "My Involvement with the PEI Ark."

51 New Alchemy Institute, *An Ark for Prince Edward Island: A Report,* "Part 1: The Ark," 23; John Todd, letter to Hussein Saleh, Environment Canada, 02 June 1976 (Earle Barnhart papers); "New Alchemy Institute (PEI) Preliminary Budget Estimate for Continuing Research Program, Ark for Prince Edward Island," n.d. [June 1976], 2-3 (Earle Barnhart papers). The Report project timeline notes under December 1975: "viii. Ark research to receive two-year support through Federal-Provincial agreement." New Alchemy Institute, *An Ark for Prince Edward Island: A Report,* "Part 1: The Ark," 25.

52 New Alchemy Institute, "The Ark Project: Budget Descriptions and Proposals, June 16, 1977" (Acc91-009, "The Ark (b) Proposals, Descriptions, Schedules 2000-7, 1977-78, Series 5.2 General Files, IMR Fonds, PEI Archive). The expensive microcomputer became an easy target for hostile critics, who (falsely) claimed that the computer was needed to run the systems and presented this as "proof" that the Ark could not be managed by an "ordinary family." Trim, "An Ark for the Future," 166-167.

53 Willis interview, 18 September 2015.

54 MacEachern, *The Institute of Man and Resources*, 57. However, the 1979 Technical Review report (discussed below) affirmed the New Alchemists' contention that "the project was clearly under-funded." See R.W. Durie, "Technical Review Meeting: Ark for Prince Edward Island, 18 January 1979," 1 (New Alchemy Vertical File, University of Prince Edward Island Special Collections).

55 An NAI PEI Board meeting on 27 March 1978 documented its "agreement with the proposal to transfer the Ark" to IMR, with a list of ten requests and stipulations regarding equipment, staff, and publication rights. An appended inventory of equipment and furniture,

stipulating what belonged to New Alchemy and what belonged to the Ark (and now to IMR), symbolized the growing separation; the file includes a handwritten note from John Todd dated 8 September 1978 confirming the ownership of "the rug" (Acc91-009, "Greenhouse (General + Mud Storage) 7.3, 1975-79, 5.2 General Files, IMR Fonds, PEI Archive).

56 D.M. Catmur, "The Prince Edward Island Centre for 'Applied Studies in Self-Sufficiency," [confidential report to IMR Director], 5 March 1978 (Acc91-009, "The Ark (b) Proposals, Descriptions, Schedules 2000-7, 1977-78, Series 5.2 General Files, IMR Fonds, PEI Archive).

57 "Ark – IMR" Vertical File (Solsearch Project Files, BGHJ Architects).

58 *The Institute of Man and Resources – Year End Report 1978* (Charlottetown: The Institute of Man and Resources, 1978), 23.

59 MacEachern, *The Institute of Man and Resources*, 57.

60 *The Institute of Man and Resources – Year End Report 1980* (Charlottetown: The Institute of Man and Resources, 1980), 11; The Ark Project, *The Year in Review* (January 1981): 6.

61 Durie, "Technical Review" (1979): 3.

62 Durie, "Technical Review" (1979): 2.

63 Durie, "Technical Review" (1979): 5.

64 IMR Year in review 1978: 4-5. *The Institute of Man and Resources – Year End Report 1980* (Charlottetown: The Institute of Man and Resources, 1980), 11; The Ark Project, *The Year in Review* (January 1981): 4-5.

65 Don J. Lahey, "Headway on the Ark: Updating Techniques for Survival," *Canadian Heritage* (02, 1981): 37-38; Linda Gilkeson and Susan Mahoney, "The Solar Salad Bar," *Harrowsmith* 33, v5 n5 (February 1981): 46-57; Susan Mahoney, ed., *A Collection of the Ark's Monthly Columns from Rural Delivery* (Souris, PE: The Ark Project, [1981]); Kenneth MacKay, "Exploration of the Self-sufficiency of the P.E.I. Ark," address to the International Conference on Basic Techniques in Ecological Agriculture, International Federation of Organic Agriculture Movements, 02-04 October 1978; K.T. MacKay and David Bergmark, "Solar Energy at the P.E.I. Ark," (Souris, PE: The Ark Project, 1978) ("The Ark – IMR" Vertical File, Solsearch Project Files, BGHJ Architects).

66 IMR's work on policy and practices mixed low profile efforts, including house insulation, systems retrofits, and energy systems, and high profile projects such as the design and construction of a cul-de-sac of five energy-efficient house prototypes. These can be seen as forerunners to the national R-2000 homes program; plans were sold to consumers at low cost. IMR's other tangible legacies are major contributions to the development of high-efficiency wood stoves and wood pellet stoves and burners, the partially-realized district energy network for Charlottetown, and continuing research since

1981 into wind power at the Atlantic Wind Test Site at North Cape (now the Wind Energy Institute of Canada). Andy Wells served as IMR Executive Director until 1984, working to change Island habits and expectations. The collapse of world energy prices in 1985 followed on the departure of Wells' energy and vision, and IMR was largely dormant beyond its fairly passive role in wind energy development at the test site. MacEachern, *The Institute of Man and Resources*, 109. IMR was finally closed in 2013. Mary MacKay, "The End of an Eco-era," Charlottetown *Guardian*, 14 January 2013, http://www.theguardian.pe.ca/Living/2013-01-14/article-3155951/The-end-of-an-eco-era/1.

67 I.A. Stewart, Deputy Minister, Energy Mines and Resources Canada, letter to J.B Seaborn, Deputy Minister, Environment Canada, 17 July 1979; J. Blair Seaborn, letter to I.A. Stewart, 24 August 1979 (Acc91-009, Background (Phasing out of Ark) 7.1, 1974-1981, Series 5.2 General Files, IMR Fonds, PEI Archives).

68 MacEachern, *The Institute of Man and Resources*, 102.

69 The Ark Project, "The Ark Project to Close," draft of newsletter article, ca. March 1981; The Ark Project, letter to staff and supporters, April 1981(Acc91-009, Background (Phasing out of Ark) 7.1, 1974-1981, Series 5.2 General Files, IMR Fonds, PEI Archives).

70 Barry Clark interview, Katherine Jones, reporter, "Ark Future" segment, *CBC News* television programme (28 January 1981; Charlottetown: CBC Television).

71 Editorial, *Eastern Graphic*, 11 January 1978; Robert Tuck's accompanying editorial cartoon is especially snide, with a shower of money raining down on the Ark from the "Federal Government" while a caricature of John Todd talks about living only on renewable resources. See also MacEachern, *The Institute of Man and Resources*, 52; Trim, "An Ark for the Future," 168.

72 Marian Bruce, "Floods of Changes at the Ark," *Atlantic Insight* (September 1980): 28-29; David Miller, "Beached! An Ark Hits Sinking Sand," Toronto *Sunday Star* (2 August 1981): A14; Trim, "An Ark for the Future," 166-167. Bruce repeats Barry Clark's claims of "trickery" perpetrated on Islanders by outsiders. Discussing the Ark's pending closure, Silver Donald Cameron also repeats the claim of total system failures, while noting that the Ark employed 11 year-round and 24 summer staff. Cameron, "The Foundering of the Ark," *Macleans* Magazine (01 June 1981): 13-14.

73 "Display ad 32 – no title," *Globe and Mail*, 31 March 1982, B6.

74 Solsearch Architects, *The Ark Park: Provincial Campground and Ecology Centre* (Charlottetown: Solsearch Architects, [1981]), 4 ("Ark Park," Solsearch Project Files, BGHJ Architects).

75 Norma Lee MacLeod, reporter, "Ark Future" segment, *Compass*

television programme (22 September 1986; Charlottetown: CBC Television).

76 John Todd interview, in Mary O'Connell, "Was Small Beautiful?" *Ideas*, radio program (16 March 2004; Toronto: Canadian Broadcasting Corporation). In Appropriate Technology terms, the demise of both the Ark and the IMR show the disjuncture between AT as a *mode of technology-practice*, and AT as a catalogue of particular, enabling technologies. The success (or failure) of the specific instances reflect upon the mode of practice as a whole; when AT groups invest heavily in specific technologies, their social-political implications tend to recede into the background (Willoughby, 334-35). Alan MacEachern notes that both New Alchemy and IMR started out to incite social change, but ended up being preoccupied by managing the development of specific techniques. MacEachern, *The Institute of Man and Resources*, 35.

77 New Alchemy Institute, *An Ark for Prince Edward Island* (1975), 1, 3. For an interpretation of the Ark as a "spaceship approach" see Henry Trim, "Experts at Work: The Canadian State, North American Environmentalism, and Renewable Energy in an Era of Limits, 1968-1983" (PhD dissertation, University of British Columbia, 2014), 157; 164-166; 175-178; Trim, "An Ark for the Future," 165-166. Trim builds his interpretation of the Ark as an instance of "cabin ecology" on analysis in Peder Anker, *From Bauhaus to Ecohouse: A History of Ecological Design* (Baton Rouge: Louisiana State University Press, 2010), 84-89, 109-112. As I argue here, the New Alchemists' presentation of the Ark as a "space ship" and "self-sufficient" was a short-lived and over-simplified representation; their commitment to participatory social change and community integration was more to the point.

78 Todd, "Tomorrow is Our Permanent Address," 103.

79 Hatchery operator Davis first tried to sell the Ark and the Spry Point site out from under the province, advertising it as an "Atlantic Retreat" in the real estate section of the *Globe and Mail* in 1985. The province intervened, deemed that Davis had not fulfilled the requirements (in terms of maintenance and hatchery production) that would allow him to purchase the Ark outright for $1 at the end of his lease in 1986, and took back the site. MacEachern, *The Institute of Man and Resources*, 110; Iris Phillips, "Spry Point Ark Not For Sale," Charlottetown *Guardian*, 28 September 1985; Norma Lee MacLeod, reporter, "Ark Future" segment, *Compass* television programme (22 September 1986; Charlottetown: CBC Television).

80 This grapevine was provided by Van Kampen's Greenhouses in Charlottetown. Jackalina Van Kampen, "Delivering a Grapevine," *The PEI Ark Online Catalogue*, last modified 25 October 2016, http://peiark.com/2016/10/delivering-a-grape-vine/. Van Kampen and his son are seen delivering the vine to Nancy Willis at the Ark in Dorothy Todd Hénaut, *Sun, Wind, and Wood*, film (1977; Montreal: National Film Board of Canada).

81 Steve Sharratt, "Group Files Objection to Awarding of Ark Parcel," Charlottetown *Guardian*, 16 September 1999, A3

82 Steve Sharratt, "High Quality Inn Rises on Site of Former Ark," Charlottetown *Guardian*, 14 March 2000, A3. The Inn's design was by Guimond + Associates Architects. At the moment of the Ark's demolition, this firm was merging with Jones & Manning Architects and Bergmark & Hammarlund Architects to form BGHJ Architects. David Bergmark, email to author, 03 March 2017.

83 Todd and Todd, *From Eco-cities to Living Machines* 11-12. In 1978, Margaret Mead directly encouraged the Todds to bring the work of New Alchemy to a broader public, and to shift the scale of their bioshelter explorations from the individual building to the scale of neighbourhoods and communities; this led to the "Village as Solar Ecology" design conference hosted by New Alchemy in 1979. Nancy Jack Todd, "Prologue," in Todd and Nancy Jack Todd, eds, *The Village as Solar Ecology*, 7.

84 On the cultural significance of the destruction of buildings, see Mannell, "Modern Heritage and Folk Culture in Atlantic Canada," 86-88; Mannell, "The Dream (and Lie) of Progress," 98, 101-102; Robert Bevan, *The Destruction of Memory: Architecture at War* (London: Reaktion, 2007), 7-8; George Orwell, "Looking Back at the Spanish Civil War," *New Road* (1943). The Ark inspired a number of projects in Atlantic Canada, though most were domestic scale and focused principally on the use of renewable energy for meeting building energy needs. Federal policy and programs also encouraged energy conservation and renewables, for example the Low-Energy Building Design Awards (LEBDA) of 1978. Interest in building-integrated solar and renewables diminished after 1980, and abruptly ended with the collapse of energy prices in 1985. Some of the building energy legacy has been picked up since the Rio Earth Summit of 1992 and the increasing concern about the major contribution of the built environment to world carbon emissions and climate change.

85 New Alchemy Institute, *An Ark for Prince Edward Island: A Report*, "Part 1: The Ark," 3.

86 Mirko Zardini, "Think Different," *Out of Gas*, 48. Zardini's "harm reduction" analysis builds on Slavoj Žižek's critique of contemporary consumerist aspirations to take the harm out of indulgences. Slavoj Žižek, *Welcome to the Desert of the Real* (London: Verso, 2002), 10-11.

87 Todd, "Tomorrow is Our Permanent Address," 41.

88 In the twentieth century, World's Fairs provided one venue for the realization of visionary and transformative architecture. Expo '67 in

Montreal was perhaps the most thorough example, with site planning and infrastructure even more radical than most of the buildings, and with Moshe Safdie's student thesis built as Habitat 67.

89 Sean Wellesley-Miller and Day Chahroudi, with Marguerite Villecco, "Bioshelter," *Architecture Plus* (November-December 1974): 90-95; Peter Harper and Godfrey Boyle, *Radical Technology* (London: Undercurrents, 1976).

90 Richard Thomas, in Hénaut, *Sun, Wind, and Wood*.

Chapter 5 Coda: The Cape Cod Ark

1 Nancy Jack Todd, "Opening the Arks," *Journal of the New Alchemists* 4 (1977): 10.

2 David Bergmark, interview by author, 05 July 2016.

3 Solsearch Architects and New Alchemy Institute, *Cape Cod Ark* poster (Woods Hole, MA: New Alchemy Institute, [1977]), gives a detailed description with drawings.

4 Ole Hammarlund, email to author, 27 July 2016.

5 Bergmark interview, 05 July 2016; Hammarlund email, 27 July 2016.

6 Nancy Jack Todd, "Opening the Arks," 11.

7 The Staff of New Alchemy & Solsearch Architects, "From Our Experience: The First Three Years Aboard the Cape Cod Ark," *Journal of the New Alchemists* 6 (1980): 113-154.

8 Earle Barnhart and Hilde Maingay, interview by author, 14 May 2015; Site visit by author, 14-15 May 2015.

Image Credits

Every effort has been made to identify those responsible for the images included in this volume.

Bill Anders/ NASA. Photographer: Bill Anders: 2.02

Earle Barnhart and Hilde Maingay. Photographer: Hilde Maingay: 1.04; 1.05; 1.06; 1.07, 1.08, 3.04, 3.27, 3.29

Earle Barnhart & Hilde Maingay: 2.15, 2.16, 3.12

David Bergmark. Photographers: Janet and David Bergmark: 1.30, 6.01

Bermark Guimond Hammarlund Jones Architects: 4.23

Bergmark & Hammarlund Architects: 4.21

Confederation Centre Art Gallery (CCAG): 2.19, 7.01, 7.02

David Falconer / EPA/ US National Archives. Photographer: David Falconer: 2.03

David and Francesca Gregori. Photograph: CCAG: 4.19

Hammarlund & Lips Architects. Photographer: Karen Lips: 4.14

John Leroux. Photographer: John Leroux: 6.02

Nancy Willis: front cover, 0.04, 1.02, 1.03, 1.09, 3.24, 4.01, 4.02, 4.05, 4.06, 4.07, 4.11, 4.12, 4.13, 4.24

Nancy Willis. Photographer: Hilde Maingay: 3.09

One Thousand Flowers Productions. Capture from video by Millefiore Clarks: 6.03

Patrick Lefebvre: 1.18, 1.19, 1.20

Public Archives of Prince Edward Island: 3.02

Simon Productions. Photographer: Peter Simon: 2.01, 2.08, 2.09, 2.13, 3.10, 5.01

Solsearch Architects. Photograph: CCAG: 2.10, 2.11

Solsearch Architects. Photographer: Fausta Hammarlund: 1.01, 1.24, 3.01, 3.22, back cover

Solsearch Architects: 0.01, 0.02, 0.03, 1.10, 1.11, 1.12, 1.13, 1.14, 1.15, 1.16, 1.17, 1.21, 1.22, 1.23, 1.25, 1.26, 1.27, 1.28, 1.29, 2.07, 2.12, 2.17, 2.18, 2.20, 3.03, 3.05, 3.06, 3.07, 3.08, 3.11, 3.13, 3.14, 3.15, 3.16, 3.17. 3.18, 3.19, 3.20, 3.21, 3.25, 3.26, 3.28, 3.35, 3.36, 4.03, 4.04, 4.08, 4.09, 4.10, 4.15, 4.16, 4.17, 4.18, 4.22, 4.25, 4.26, 4.27, 5.02, 5.03

Steven Mannell. Photographer: Steven Mannell: 2.04, 2.05, 2.06, 3.02, 3.23, 4.20

Toronto Reference Library: 2.14

Acknowledgments

Lukas Bergmark was the catalyst for the two years of collaboration that led to this book, the exhibition, and the website. Lukas had just finished his architecture degree at Dalhousie in late summer 2014 when he called me for advice on finding "someone" who might be interested in putting the Ark properly into the scholarly and public record. His essay in this book is clear about his motivation. His timing was optimal, coming early in my 2014-15 sabbatical, and the concept aligned with my half-formed notion of studying the emergence of "ecological architecture" in the 1970s. Lukas had an important ally in Silva Stojack of BGHJ Architects, who pledged substantial in-kind support for cataloguing and documenting the office's extensive drawings and files related to the Ark and other Solsearch projects. Early financial support was provided by a sabbatical leave grant from Dalhousie University, and funds from the Dalhousie Student Employment Program for Coop Students. Major financial support for research and for the presentation of the exhibition was provided by the Canada Council.

David Bergmark and Ole Hammarlund had the good grace to respond enthusiastically when the project was presented to them, and added a real zing to the project in agreeing to rebuild the original Ark systems model on film. Nancy Willis was a generous source of anecdotes and photographs, and provided a personal and social texture to the story. David, Ole and Nancy gave limitless time and attention to the research, spending time in conversation and interviews, digging out photographs and files, reading drafts of the text for fact checking, and responding to innumerable last-minute email messages checking details. The richness of the story is largely due to their openness and energy over the past 2-1/2 years. The Ark marked a deeply personal defining moment for all three, and I hope my efforts bear out my respect for their contributions.

Other participants in the Ark story also made important contributions. Earle Barnhart and Hilde Maingay made me welcome overnight at the Cape Cod Ark, and took me through their extensive files with an entertaining and enlightening commentary on the place of the Ark within the work of the New Alchemy Institute; they also shared their files and Hilde's wonderful photographs for the exhibition and book, and Earle answered numerous questions in detail. Bruce McCallum's contribution to the "share your story" section of the PEIArk.com website offered a look into the environmentalist circles within government in the mid-1970s. Lynne Douglas made useful suggestions and corrections to chapters 2 and 4; Alex Campbell also reviewed these for general accuracy. John Todd provided some key clarifications and insights by email.

Creating the exhibition, book, and website was a joyful process of collaboration. Kevin Rice and Pan Wendt at the Confederation Centre Art Gallery were enthusiastic and supportive of the proposed exhibition. Michelangelo Sabatino saw the relevance of the Ark research to the Dalhousie Architectural Press *Canadian Modern* series, and helped frame the book as a comprehensive companion to the exhibition, and more than just a catalogue. Millefiore Clarkes of One Thousand Flowers Production created a film for the website and exhibition showing David and Ole sharing reminiscences forty years later while rebuilding the lost systems model. Brad and Karen Trivers of Sunrise Web built the website for the PEI Ark Online Catalogue, www.PEIArk.com, enabling ongoing sharing of research and stories throughout the research.

The Dalhousie School of Architecture's summer 2016 Free Lab course offered a chance to collaborate with students in developing the curatorial approach, and resulted in important elements of the exhibition and book. Justin Chetty and Matei Rau developed the influence map and timeline; Jennifer Kalman and Wenhao Li created a set of "all ages" system diagrams; Patrick Lefebvre constructed the detailed digital model of the Ark, and later went far beyond the call of duty in creating a powerful animation video along with the diagrams reproduced in chapter 1. Kelly Cameron, Ryan Swirsky and Gregory Urquhart created a pair of viewport dioramas based on original photographs to create a more vivid visual sense of life in the Ark. The full-scale mockup of the Ark kitchen/ kitchen greenhouse space was designed and components fabricated by Christopher Barss, Luke Godden, Bilal Khan, and Marie Macinnis.

David Bergmark, Lukas Bergmark, and Ole Hammarlund provided several last-minute days of design-build work to complete the mock-up for the exhibition, assisted by New Alchemist Albert Doolittle, who led the creation of an in-situ demonstration of Suntube aquaculture. David Keller of Kalwall Corporation provided the Suntube ponds, while Everett Barber of Sunworks loaned an original solar collector panel. Dalhousie Architecture students David Burlock and Lucas McDowell fabricated the mixed-media architectural models for the exhibition, under the direction of Megan Peck. The staff of the Confederation Centre Art Gallery were a joy to work with, bearing the last-minute preparations and installation with remarkable grace and goodwill. I am also grateful to the staff of the College of Sustainability, who put up with a very distracted Director for much of the six months prior to the opening, and to my SUST 1000 co-instructor John Bingham, who covered for me without complaint (and often without much notice).

Though I was aware of the PEI Ark as a teenager vaguely considering a career in architecture, I must confess that the Ark had entirely left my awareness by the time I was established as a professor at Dalhousie's School of Architecture in the late 1990s. Credit for my reawakened interest and subsequent research is due to architect William MacCallum, the Newfoundland and Labrador representative on the *Atlantic Modern* jury in 2001, who reminded us of the Ark and its regional, national, and international significance and insisted that the Ark be included in the exhibition and book. I continued to study and write about the Ark in the context of modern heritage challenges over the next few years. In 2009, my appointment as Director of Dalhousie's new interdisciplinary College of Sustainability led to a significant shift in my teaching, now focused on broad issues of sustainability and social change. The Ark now offered a bridge between architecture and sustainability, and I used it as centrepiece of a lecture in our first year introductory sustainability course.

Claire Campbell, my co-instructor and co-author of SUST 1000, introduced me to the world of environmental history, and invited Alan MacEachern as a guest lecturer. We had a great time improvising a joint lecture on the Ark and the Institute of Man and Resources for the course in the Fall of 2009; this led me to participate in a week-long environmental history conference "A Time and a Place" organized by Alan and Irene Novaczek in June 2010 where, among a feast of collegial pleasures, I met George McRobie and heard his take on the Ark, the IMR, and the PEI scene in the late 1970s. Once the present book and exhibition project was conceived, Alan's book on the IMR was an important tool, enabling me to locate the Ark in policy and social contexts; our conversations suggested meaningful ways forward for further analysis. Henry Trim's dissertation and articles added breadth and detail; Hank also provided copies of several crucial but hard-to-find articles and documents. Wade McLaughlin's biography of Alex Campbell fleshed out another key realm of detail and context. Conversations with Michelangelo Sabatino and Pan Wendt led me to Daniel Barber, whose scholarship linking architectural and environmental histories is vivid and instructive. I am very grateful for Daniel's fine introduction, situating the Ark in its environmental-architectural context.

Special thanks to those groups and individuals who provided venues for sharing work in progress on this project, and for their insightful comments and suggestions on those occasions. Francine Vanlaethem, Martin Drouin, and Marie-Dina Salvione's invitation to the Docomomo Quebec Study Day in 2014 instigated the first public airing of this research and analysis. Presentations to the Association for Critical Heritage Studies, the Saskatchewan Association of Architects, the Architects Association of Prince Edward Island, and the Canadian Green Building Council Atlantic Chapter provided responses from diverse academic and professional perspectives. Kim Förster at the Canadian Centre for Architecture enabled a useful day-long exchange with Power Corporation residency students Lisa Chow, Michèle Curtis, and Geneviève Depelteau in 2016. My students in sustainability (SUST 1000) and architectural history and theory (ARCH 3105) helped keep me honest and clear in my claims. And my good colleagues at the Society for the Study of Architecture in Canada/ Société pour l'étude de l'architecture au Canada annual meetings listened attentively and responded critically to the research over several years, always offering a receptive and welcoming home for speculation.

The final text has been improved by the careful attention of a number of readers. Laureen van Lierop, Megan Peck, and Susanne Marshall read the earliest drafts; John Leroux and Stephen Parcell were the formal peer reviewers; David Bergmark and Ole Hammarlund read the pre- and post-review versions to verify facts and interpretation; and Christine Macy read the final draft. Thank you all.

Thanks also to the many others who provided materials or guidance along the way, including Barry Ahmad, National Film Board of Canada; Jack Alarie; Richie Allen, Library and Archives Canada; Anne Bergmark; Linda Berko, PEI Museum and Heritage Foundation; Amy Bishop, Iowa State University; John Boylan, PEI Public Archives; Laurie Brinklow, UPEI; Lindsay Brown, Habitat76.ca; Satadal Dasgupta, UPEI; Emily Dingwall, Library and Archives Canada; Phil Ferraro; Adam Gallant, The Hill Sound Studio; Peter Hall, CBC; Wayne Henning, CBC; Ken Kam, Dalhousie University; James Lawrence; Brian Lilley, Dalhousie University; Karen Lips; Jocelyne Lloyd, The Charlottetown *Guardian*; Simon Lloyd, UPEI; Alan MacEachern, Western University; Barbi McGuigan, CBC; Lea Nakonechny, National Film Board of Canada; Tim Noakes, Stanford University; Reg Peters, Dalhousie University; Anita Regan, Dalhousie University; Paul Ryan, SABIC Polymershapes; Daniel Shoemaker, Piedmont Plastics; Peter Simon, Simon Productions; Barry Smith, Nova Scotia Public Archives; Regan Southcott, Dalhousie University; Lionel Stevenson, Camera Art Limited; John Versteege, Impact Videographic; Alan Walker, Toronto Reference Library; Darren Yearsly, CBC.

Finally, a special note of profound gratitude to the two powerful women who were instrumental in driving the project through its final year.

Megan Peck was a research assistant beyond all reasonable expectations, acting as steady engine of project tasks, cold calls, material sourcing, and sweet-talking people into providing what was needful. She rose to the task of guiding the day-to-day work of a dozen students in the summer 2016 Free Lab, which produced a substantial part of the curatorial material, and topped that by managing the production of three amazing architectural models, delivered safely through torrential rain to arrive just in time for the exhibition opening. Her quiet editorial hand and the deep knowledge of the Ark she developed over a year's immersion have shaped the text for the better.

Laureen van Lierop, my best friend, wife, and partner, always my trusted first reader, has been a believer in the Ark vision since she saw the *Chatelaine* article as a young woman. Her commitment to the beauty of the Ark idea, and her commitment to me, kept me going on a project I care deeply about, through a year beset by especially difficult personal challenges. This book is dedicated to her dedication.

Notes on Contributors

Project Team

Author/Exhibition Curator
Steven Mannell, Dalhousie University

Assistant Curator
Lukas Bergmark

Research and Curatorial Assistant
Megan Peck

Collaborators
David Bergmark, Solsearch Architects
Ole Hammarlund, Solsearch Architects
Nancy Willis, New Alchemy Institute
Earle Barnhart, New Alchemy Institute
Hilde Maingay, New Alchemy Institute
Silva Stojack, BGHJ Architects
Kevin Rice, Confederation Centre Art Gallery
Pan Wendt, Confederation Centre Art Gallery

Biographies

Steven Mannell, NSAA, FRAIC, is founding Director of Dalhousie University's College of Sustainability. He is a practicing architect and Professor of Architecture. His research includes the architecture of public works, the documentation and conservation of modern built heritage, and the emergence of "ecological architecture" in the 1970s. He is author of *Atlantic Modern: The Architecture of the Atlantic Provinces 1950-2000* (2004).

Daniel A. Barber is an Assistant Professor of Architecture at the University of Pennsylvania School of Design. He is a historian and theorist with a research interest in the relationship between developments in architecture and the emergence of global environmental culture during the 20th century, and author of *A House in the Sun: Modern Architecture and Solar Energy in the Cold War* (2016).

Lukas Bergmark initiated this exhibition and book project while practicing at BGHJ Architects under the mentorship of his father, David Bergmark. Currently, Lukas practices at KPMB Architects, specializing in envelope design for institutional projects. Before acquiring his Master of Architecture degree from Dalhousie University, he studied Art History and Cultural Studies at McGill University.

Back cover: Solsearch Architects: Ole Hammarlund and David Bergmark, 1975.